Orkney and Shetland:

An Archaeological Guide

Orkney and Shetland:

An Archaeological Guide

Lloyd Laing

DAVID & CHARLES

NEWTON ABBOT   LONDON

NORTH POMFRET (VT)   VANCOUVER

ISBN o 7153 6305 o
© Lloyd Laing 1974

Set in 11 on 13pt Imprint
and printed in Great Britain by
Latimer Trend & Company Ltd Plymouth
for David & Charles (Holdings) Limited
South Devon House Newton Abbot Devon

Published in the United States of America
by David & Charles Inc North Pomfret
Vermont 05053 USA

Published in Canada
by Douglas David & Charles Limited
3645 McKechnie Drive West Vancouver BC

Contents

List of Illustrations

PLATES

FIGURES

9

Preface

With the possible exception of Wessex, the Northern Isles are archaeologically the richest and most varied region of the British Isles. Each
year sees an increase in the number of visitors to the islands, yet at
present there is no general guide to the archaeology of Orkney and
Shetland written for the non-specialist which brings into account the
important developments in archaeological thinking that have taken
place during the last ten years. The only general survey attempted,
F. T. Wainwright's *The Northern Isles* (1962), is now both very out-
dated and too detailed for the average visitor.

During the period 1966–9 when I was employed as assistant inspec-
tor of Ancient Monuments with the then Ministry of Public Building
& Works, I had the fortune to have special responsibilities for the
monuments in the Northern Isles. I felt then that a general book was
needed, and began this in 1968, but was prevented from completing it
by pressures of work. An opportunity presented itself to return to the
Isles in 1972, and following this the book was totally rewritten in that
year.

Although written mainly for the visitor, for whom a gazetteer has
been included of sites to visit, it is hoped that it will also be of interest
to the 'armchair archaeologist'. For those wishing to find out more
about the subject than the scope of this book permits, a list of Further
Reading is included, listing the most important books and articles
published since about 1962 (the date of publication of Wainwright's
book) together with some more general works of reference.

L. L.

Chronology

Until the early 1950s the dates used for the cultures of prehistoric Europe and Britain were arrived at by a complex and often tenuous series of correlations with the civilised world of the East Mediterranean, for which written history and a few absolute dates were available from around 3000 BC.

After World War II it was discovered that one of the radioactive isotopes of carbon decays at a fixed rate for a period of roughly 5,500 years, the decay starting to take place at the point at which the carbon ceases to be part of a living organism absorbing further carbon from the atmosphere. After 5,500 years the decay becomes irregular, and cannot be measured precisely.

In the 1950s and 1960s a chronological scheme was worked out for European prehistory on the basis of a wide range of radiocarbon dates. Unfortunately it was not realised that the dates arrived at were not calendrically accurate in all cases, some dates appearing very much later than they should have due to geophysical factors. This only became apparent when a study of the dates provided by the growth rings of certain types of very long-lived trees, notably the American bristlecone pine, drew attention to the anomaly, the bristlecone pine dates corresponding very closely with the historical dates known from the Near East.

It would appear, then, that conventional radiocarbon dates for British prehistory are too late. Nevertheless, it was felt that in the present state of debate over prehistoric chronology it was unwise to adopt here a scheme of dating based on dates recalibrated from bristle-cone pine, especially since a radiocarbon chronology is lacking for the Northern Isles and there is still only a limited number of dates available for Scotland as a whole. For convenience, a table of recalibrated dates is here given:

Conventional Radiocarbon Date	Recalibrated Date
3000 BC	3710 BC
2500	3250
2000	2490
1750	2140
1500	1720
1250	1510
1000	1330–1230
800	980–890
700	870
600	790
500	530
400	460
300	400
200	330
150	150

The above dates are based on those published by Dr Hugh McKerrell in 'Some Aspects of the Accuracy of Carbon-14 Dating', *Scottish Archaeological Forum*, 3 (1971), 73–84.

CHAPTER I

The Land and the People

Today, the visitor to the Northern Isles crossing by ferry from the north of Scotland inadvertently follows the route of the earliest settlers nearly 5,000 years ago. Apart from the few scattered towns and villages, the land is remarkably unchanged by modern man, a factor which has allowed the survival of more ancient monuments per square mile in the Islands than anywhere else in Britain.

Orkney, except for the rugged cliffs of Hoy, is gentle and undulating, with few hills and rich farmland, a landscape that reflects centuries of peaceful cultivation. Although it has much in common with the mainland of Caithness, it lacks the uninhabited stretches of peat bog so characteristic there. Shetland, in contrast, is wild and stormy. There are few rich farms, and the landscape is dominated by moorland and machar. Orkney is perhaps best symbolised by the soft red sandstone of St Magnus' Cathedral; Shetland, by the forbidding defences of the Hanoverian Fort Charlotte.

Geology

The geography of the Northern Isles—rock formations, profile, soil—has contributed as much to their character as the exploits of man.

The Orkney islands are primarily composed of Devonian Old Red Sandstone, with some older granites and schists round Stromness on Mainland and a few outcrops of basaltic lavas on Hoy. The Devonian sandstones are soft and erode rapidly—the Old Man, the famous column of sandstone off the south-west coast of Hoy, is probably the

product of erosion during the last two centuries—and many sites on cliffs show signs of having been extensively eroded in the last 2,000 years. The present gentle contours of the landscape are in part due to the retreat of the main ice sheet northwards in the Ice Age. Hoy had a local icefield, and glacial moraines from it can be recognised on Ward Hill. The Old Red Sandstones contain flagstones and conglomerates which are clearly bedded and jointed and split off along the bedding plane into slabs. This results in the spectacularly stepped appearance of the shorelines or other exposed outcrops. The facility with which the stone can be split into slabs makes it ideal for building, and nature as well as human skill is responsible for the very high standard displayed in Orkney monuments. The availability of suitable stone, together with the shortage of timber, led Orcadian builders from prehistoric times onwards to use stone where normally they would have used wood. This has caused the fortunate preservation of sites like Skara Brae, where even the furnishings were of stone slabs.

In Shetland few of the rocks produce slabs suitable for building, though there are outcrops of Old Red Sandstone in the south-east, round Sandsting, and in Foula. Most of the rocks in Shetland are extremely metamorphosed, major thrust zones running across the islands. The Shetland landscape too has been affected by glacial action, with local icefields on Ronas Hill and Delting, as well as the ice streams from Norway. The dissimilar geology results in the Shetland monuments differing from the Orcadian ones: structures in Shetland appear cruder and less carefully constructed, though the Iron Age monuments can be architecturally almost as accomplished. The greater dearth of good arable land in Shetland is emphasised by the different distribution pattern of human settlement there.

Human settlement in Orkney and Shetland

The visitor to Orkney and Shetland is impressed most by the extent of human settlement in antiquity in this remote area, and by the remarkable character of the islands' culture. To some extent this impression is more apparent than real, for historical accident has led to the preservation of ancient monuments. Other areas of Britain were as densely populated in antiquity, but remains have been destroyed by industrial and urban development, forestry, ploughing or the spread of later villages. In most areas of the British Isles the destruction of ancient monuments on a large scale has been a fairly recent phenomenon, more having been destroyed in the last two decades than at any other time in our history, though the process has been increasing since the eighteenth century. The area that has been most affected has been the lowland zone, the rich fertile land that has been cultivated and inhabited since the time of the first Neolithic farmers. The highland zone, notably Wales, the Lake District or the Scottish Highlands, was never as conducive to early settlement, nor was the acid soil suited to the preservation of the remains of human habitation. Although sites here have been spared urban growth, industry or motorway development, they have suffered from less obvious but nevertheless important destruction factors—forestry (particularly a phenomenon of the post-World War II era) and quarrying.

Orkney, and to a lesser extent Shetland, were suited to early habitation, if not perhaps as ideally as the fertile English lowlands. Forestry and quarrying have little part in the destruction of sites in the Northern Isles, the main threats being farming or marine erosion. This last factor is an important one, for more sites have been destroyed by the sea in the Northern Isles than by any other agency. But although marine erosion is a serious problem for the archaeologist, the sea normally takes centuries to destroy what man can destroy in days.

It seems unlikely that this situation will continue indefinitely in the Northern Isles. Each summer sees an increasing influx of tourists, and if the present prediction of oil fields off the Orkney coast proves sound it will bring a new industrial prosperity to the Isles. Apart from summer visitors, more and more people are going to the Northern Isles to retreat from the tempo of urban existence. The outcome will inevitably be new housing, hotels, shops, car parks and the other amenities which will take their toll of ancient monuments.

Archaeologists in the Isles

Although the archaeological wealth of the Northern Isles is perhaps comparable with that of Wessex, Orkney attracted the attention of less accomplished antiquaries. By far the greatest proportion of the Orkney barrows and brochs were pillaged in the nineteenth century by local dilettantes and a great number of anonymous lootings occurred as well as the digging activities of local antiquaries such as William Traill and James Farrar. Few plans or records exist of these investigations.

Sites such as Skara Brae, Rinyo, Jarlshof, Broch of Gurness or the Brough of Birsay had to wait until the inter-war years for careful excavation, in a period of extensive archaeological activity, fostered in great part in Orkney by the whisky magnate Walter Grant. The same period witnessed the fieldwork of the Royal Commission on Ancient & Historic Monuments in Orkney and Shetland. The resultant three-volume *Inventory*, not published till 1948, still remains a basic source of information on the archaeology of the Isles. Other aspects of research were not disregarded: in 1938 the late Dr A. B. Taylor published his translation of the great Icelandic *Orkneyinga Saga*, and about the same time the late Dr Hugh Marwick was studying the placenames of Orkney.

The outbreak of World War II interrupted excavations at the Broch of Gurness, Birsay and Jarlshof, but after the war interest revived with the resumption of work at Jarlshof and the subsequent excavations at Clickhimin in Shetland. The discovery of the St Ninian's Isle Treasure in 1958 further attracted attention to Shetland archaeology, though the excavation at St Ninian's Isle itself was on a modest scale, as indeed have been most post-war excavations. The work begun by the Royal Commission in Shetland was carried on by one of the investigators, Mr C. S. T. Calder, but on the whole far more fieldwork has been done in Orkney over the years than in Shetland. Once the framework for the archaeology of the Northern Isles was established in the inter-war years, subsequent work tended to result in modifications of existing knowledge, though recent work on Scottish chambered tombs and the fort and broch cultures of the early Iron Age have radically altered some aspects.

The 1960s saw the opening of two museums to house and display local archaeological material. The first, at Lerwick, was originally planned to house the St Ninian's Isle Treasure, although eventually this went to the National Museum of Antiquities of Scotland in Edinburgh, and only facsimiles are now on display in Lerwick. Lerwick Museum does however house a selection of material from Jarlshof and Clickhimin (though again the best finds are in Edinburgh), as well as a general collection of important Shetland antiquities. Particularly notable in the collection are the early Christian stones from Papil, West Burra. The second museum, at Tankerness House in Kirkwall, houses an interesting well displayed collection of Orcadian antiquities, though again most of the best material is at Edinburgh in the national collection. The sixteenth-century building has been beautifully restored, and displays the collection to full advantage. The museum in Stromness is mainly devoted to natural and local history. As an off-shoot of Lerwick Museum a local society has grown up, which is engaged in profitable archaeological work in the islands.

The character of the archaeology of the Northern Isles

A remarkable characteristic of the archaeology of the Northern Isles is the insular adaptation and development of ideas and settlement types which originated elsewhere. Only for a period in the Bronze Age do the Northern Isles seem to have developed almost without external stimulus, a situation which in fact is reflected in Britain as a whole. At other times the Northern Isles seem to have been in the mainstream of Scottish cultural developments, their peoples not merely adopting new ideas from outside but modifying them into distinctive variants. Presumably due to its remoteness, Shetland appears to have seen fewer innovations than Orkney, and to have been more culturally impoverished.

A second characteristic of the islands is the cultural substratum which persisted with little change throughout their prehistory, and which belongs to a widespread tradition that archaeologists know as the 'circumpolar'. It is most apparent in Shetland, and can be recognised in the 'circumpolar tool-kit'—the basic equipment of stone mauls, pounders, pot lids, line sinkers and so on that occur at all periods—and in the range of bone tools. Iron Age tools for instance are very similar to those used by the Neolithic occupants of Skara Brae, and both show features in common with those used by the Eskimos in the more recent past. This conservatism can also be detected in the basic type of house in prehistoric Shetland, the 'courtyard house', which has a continuous history from the Neolithic to the Iron Age. Some continuity of building traditions can also be observed in Orkney. Among the peasantry, new types of objects once introduced seem to have had a long life. For instance in Shetland pottery with fluted rims was made alongside other types from its introduction in the early Iron Age up to the time of the Norse settlements.

Because of the chance survival of Neolithic sites in Shetland, tombs and houses can be related to the land units, and settlement patterns and economy studied in a way impossible elsewhere in Neolithic Britain. To a lesser extent this is also possible in Orkney; on Rousay, for example, Professor Childe demonstrated how the distribution of chambered tombs coincided with the units of arable land, one collective tomb being found in each unit. Unfortunately as yet only the two Neolithic villages of Rinyo and Skara Brae in Orkney balance the picture with that of Shetland. Most of the evidence concerns death— the archaeology of Neolithic Orkney comprises mainly the chambered tombs and their development.

The Age of Bronze

The inception of the Bronze Age heralded a cultural 'golden age' in Orkney. For a time there was great activity, with the building of the circles of standing stones at Brodgar and Stenness, linked by a processional way and surrounded by burial mounds and other standing stones. Gold mounts and amber were found in one of the mounds in the barrow cemetery known as the Knowes of Trotty, on Orkney Mainland, and it seems possible there was some connection between Orkney and the rich Wessex culture of southern England. No rich bronze-working society however emerged in either Orkney or Shetland; there are few early or middle Bronze Age objects from the islands at all, and it is possible that there was no indigenous bronze industry on any scale at least until an itinerant smith set up his workshop towards the end of the period at Jarlshof. Grave finds of the middle and late Bronze Age are meagre, and consist of crude steatite urns with cremated bones in stone cists, often inserted into earlier mounds. Little is known about the settlements of the period, and only with the advent of new peoples from the Scottish mainland in the late Bronze Age do habitation sites occur again in the Northern Isles.

Iron Age settlers

Slightly later, Iron Age settlers also colonised the Northern Isles, introducing new types of pottery and circular huts with internal partitions. They arrived in the late sixth or fifth century BC and were reinforced probably sometime after 400 BC by further immigrants whose original homeland possibly was in France, and who built at Clickhimin the first stone walled fort there. From now on the Northern Isles were to pass into a heroic period in which warfare, and probably concomitant with it a flamboyant tribal aristocracy, was to provide the colour. Farming seems to have continued, and also probably to a lesser extent fowling and fishing. Broch towers, so characteristic of the Iron Age in northern Scotland, seem to have developed from the stone forts of the Hebrides, and from there were introduced to Orkney and Shetland, where they were further developed and enlarged. Broch architecture is characteristic of the first two centuries AD. By the second century a more peaceful climate of existence was being established, and broch towers were no longer needed as forts for petty chiefs and their followers. The descendants of the original builders continued to live on the broch sites, sometimes building their wheelhouses and other small stone houses inside the brochs themselves or at their base, sometimes pillaging the stone.

The post-broch (in Shetland 'wheelhouse') period of the Iron Age continued until the arrival of the Norse at the end of the eighth century. From now on the Northern Isles were little more than a Norse colony. Some at least of the later post-broch inhabitants of the Northern Isles were Picts; there was a Pictish church at Birsay, and Pictish symbol stones and ogham inscriptions are known from the Northern Isles, while at St Ninian's Isle the famous treasure is of Pictish workmanship.

The era of the Vikings

Pagan Norse archaeology consists mainly of ninth-century graves with some ninth-century settlement sites, most notably at Jarlshof. Although the 'official' conversion of the Norse was somewhat later, they were probably in great part Christian by the later ninth century. Christian Norse remains are very varied, ranging from St Magnus' Cathedral in Kirkwall down to humbler churches like Egilsay, St Mary's on Wyre, Eynhallow, or perhaps the curious round church at Orphir built on the plan of the Church of the Holy Sepulchre at Jerusalem. A few Norse castles are known, most notably Cubbie Roo's Castle on Wyre—simple rectangular towers that are among the earliest examples of castle architecture in Scotland. Habitation sites of the period too are varied, ranging from the simple longhouse to complex structures like Earl Thorfinn's Palace at Birsay.

The twelfth century onwards

By the middle of the twelfth century the Northern Isles, and more particularly Orkney, were passing into the full flower of the Romanesque. Gradually the Isles became more oriented towards feudal Scotland and away from Norway, though they were still politically Norse. In the second quarter of the thirteenth century the Norse earls were followed by the Scottish, and political ties were finally broken in 1469 when the Isles were pledged to James III by Christian of Denmark (by this time the kingdom of Norway belonged to Denmark) as a pledge for a marriage dowry he could not raise. Subsequent attempts by Denmark to redeem the pledge failed, and technically the Northern Isles are still Scandinavian.

Until the thirteenth century Orkney and Shetland were still Norse both in language and way of life, but as time passed there was a considerable influx of followers of the Scottish earls and bishops. The medieval farmhouses of Orkney and Shetland are generally similar to the type that was current on the mainland, and are probably not derived from Norse longhouses, as has sometimes been suggested. Later medieval inhabitants of Orkney and Shetland used pottery imported from eastern Scotland and even Yorkshire.

The sixteenth century witnessed the domination of the Stewart earls, Robert and Patrick, two tyrants who oppressed their earldom. They were responsible for the building of the earls' palaces at Kirkwall and Birsay in Orkney and at Scalloway in Shetland. The castles of the sixteenth-century Northern Isles are consistent with castle architecture elsewhere on the mainland—Scalloway is a typically grim tower house, though the earl's palace at Kirkwall is a fine example of Scottish Renaissance architecture, in the tradition of Linlithgow Palace or Stirling Castle. Slightly earlier, the last vestige of Scandinavian architectural tradition had manifested itself in the bishop's palace at Kirkwall which, though its present form is sixteenth century, incorporates a thirteenth-century building in which Haakon IV of Norway died in 1263.

CHAPTER 2

Farmers and Tomb Builders

Although there is evidence that man was present in Britain long before the end of the fourth and last glaciation, perhaps as early as 270000 BC, there appears to have been no human habitation in Scotland before 5500 BC. Radiocarbon dating from sites like Morton (Fife) and Barsalloch and Low Clone (Wigtown) suggest that the first food gatherers spread into Scotland following the gradual retreat of the ice sheet, the settlers at Morton sheltering behind primitive windbreaks and living on a diet primarily consisting of fish and shellfish.

These early food gathering communities seem to have spread gradually over much of the Scottish mainland. Some seem to have reached Orkney, where a few tanged flint implements suggest that they were culturally retarded, continuing to make tools of an Upper Palaeolithic (Old Stone Age) character long after such tools had become obsolete elsewhere in Europe (Fig 3). Nothing is known of the origins of these early settlers, nor of the nature of their settlements in the Isles. There seem to be at least two separate groups, one of which has its closest parallels in West Norway, the other in France.

The first farming settlers in Orkney and Shetland do not appear to have ventured the crossing from Caithness until some time after 3000 BC at a time when communities of Neolithic farmers were well established in some parts of Scotland, while Shetland was probably settled even later.

The Neolithic era was distinguished by early antiquaries primarily as a stage of technological advance from chipped to polished stone

Fig 2 *Skara Brae, Orkney*

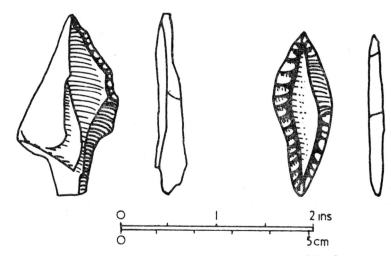

O   1   2 ins

O   5cm

Fig 3   *Mesolithic tanged points from Millfield, Stronsay, and Brodgar, Stenness, Mainland, Orkney (after Livens)*

tools. Later antiquaries characterised it by the first appearance of pottery. Since the inter-war years however it has been recognised that the most significant development was the transition from a food gathering to a food producing economy, perhaps the most momentous development in social evolution. Today, the old three-fold division of prehistoric cultures into a Stone Age, Bronze Age and Iron Age, originally put forward on the basis of the material used for edge tools, has become more or less obsolete, for improved techniques of excavation and analysis have provided prehistorians with a much wider view of earlier societies than was formerly available. But in spite of recent attempts to find substitutes, the old 'three age system' is still used by prehistorians as a convenient way of grouping material in terms of relative development, and as such is used in this book.

THE SPREAD OF NEOLITHIC MAN

The first farmers

The step forward from food gathering to food production allowed

27

men for the first time in 2 million years of existence to settle in one place sufficiently long to amass property and build villages rather than temporary shelters. Hitherto, only groups of people whose economy was entirely founded on fishing had been able to build villages, and only in such societies are a great number of material possessions to be found. The material equipment of the food gatherers was simple and underwent only slight modification over a period of time, being adequate for most needs. A nomadic society of necessity must travel unencumbered by possessions if it has to move to keep up with its food supply.

It is important to remember that the domestication of animals and the cultivation of plants could only take place where the wild species were to be found. By a strange coincidence the wild ancestors of sheep, goats, pigs, cattle, wheat and barley were to be found together only in the Near East, and it was here that farming began. The first evidence for domesticated sheep comes from Iran around 8000 BC; cattle were domesticated much later, not appearing until the fifth millennium. A single centre of domestication is improbable—pigs, which were to be found as a wild breed in much of Europe, certainly seem to have been domesticated independently in several places. In Europe the dog was domesticated as early as 7500 BC as an adjunct to hunting—and one of the earliest known was found at Star Carr in Yorkshire—but it seems to have had little effect on the food gathering economy. The main characteristic of the species of early domesticated animals was their tendency to be gregarious in the wild; once the leaders were tamed the rest of the herd followed. Domesticated animals can be recognised archaeologically by their small bones.

The deliberate planting of crops is the natural successor to the reaping of wild harvests. In Palestine wheat was probably cultivated by 8500 BC and by about 7000 BC agricultural communities were spread widely in the Near East, Palestine and Turkey. From the Near East the First Agricultural Revolution as it has been called, rapidly spread to Europe. By 6000 BC villages of farmers are found in Greece and the Balkans, with offshoots farther north on the Danube.

Except in the Near East, where the annual inundations of the rivers brought fertilising mud to the fields, the early agriculturalists rapidly exhausted the soil used for cultivation and grazing, and had to move increasingly farther from their original home. A technique of agriculture known as 'slash-and-burn' characterises these movements. As the land became exhausted the forest was cleared by cutting down trees and burning the stumps which provided ash for the cleared ground. This factor led to the rapid spread of Neolithic farmers from Greece and the Balkans to other parts of Europe, their progress being mainly up the Danube north-westwards towards the Rhine, following the fertile loess soils which probably carried a less dense forest cover and, by means of the sea, along the Mediterranean littoral. By 5000 BC there were farming communities on the Rhine. As they spread into temperate Europe the deteriorating weather conditions forced them to abandon the mud-brick flat-roofed houses which had been so suited to the Near East and east Mediterranean, the later buildings of the Neolithic settlers in central Europe being long timber trapezoidal houses with sloping roofs to throw off the rain water, large enough to accommodate several families.

In western Europe

The origins and relationships of the various early farming communities of western Europe are difficult to assess. In north Europe many of the cultural traits of the early farmers probably spread among the indigenous food gatherers, and this phenomenon probably accounts for the mixed character of the Neolithic cultures of France, the Low Countries and the British Isles. The Danubians (frequently called 'linear pottery' cultures on account of the characteristic decorative device used on their pottery) did not extend further than Poland and the Low Countries. In France and the Iberian peninsula the first farmers were of Mediterranean stock, characterised by pottery decorated with the impressions of cardium shells. These people of the 'cardial' or 'impressed ware' cultures played an important part in the development of the later Neolithic societies of France.

One of the problems in attempting to assess the origins of the first farming communities in the British Isles lies in the fact that we have very little information about the first settlers, who probably arrived in southern England around the middle to late fourth millennium BC. Their presence is attested not so much by archaeological as by botanical evidence, for the advent of early farmers seems to have been accompanied by a marked decline in the growth of elm trees, due to the leaves being stripped for animal fodder. This elm decline, which can be gauged by the decrease in elm pollen in peat bogs and other deposits, seems to have been a widespread phenomenon in north Europe. It seems to have taken place around 3000 BC or somewhat earlier, as radiocarbon dates from sites as widely separated as Shippea Hill in Cambridgeshire and Ehenside Tarn in the Lake District attest. This practice characterises the phase of *landnam* or land-taking, as does the absence of recognisable settlements, and it must be presumed that the early settlers in this country lived in houses of a flimsy nature that have left no traces for archaeologists. The most substantial remains are grain-storage pits (which were later filled with rubbish), the distribution of which extends over much of lowland Britain. Initially, the settlements of the colonists in Britain would have been scattered and mainly coastal, gradually spreading inland. One possible settlement type in this *landnam* phase was a lakeside or coastal settlement of timber dwellings—there are hints that such settlements once existed at Shippea Hill, Ehenside Tarn, and Storrs Moss in Lancashire—and these have their counterparts in north-central Europe.

Pottery is usually a useful clue to the origins of prehistoric communities, but unfortunately in the case of early Neolithic Britain the affinities of the earliest pottery cannot be localised to any one area of Europe. The pottery from Hembury in Dorset, which seems to be among the earliest from the British Isles, has its closest counterparts in Normandy, but other examples appear to be more closely related to the wares current among the Michelsberg culture of the Low Countries and Germany.

The primary phase of Neolithic Britain is usually termed the Windmill Hill culture after a site near Avebury in Wiltshire. This classic site is not as early as places like Hembury, and the culture is distinguished by coarse, handmade pottery with leathery, bag-shaped forms, some of which reflect Michelsberg, others Chassey (north France) forms. The Windmill Hill culture spread over southern England, and has other characteristic attributes, such as 'causewayed camps'. Windmill Hill itself is an example of one of these earthworks which consist of ditches broken by gaps or causeways. The Windmill Hill people also seem to have been responsible for opening up complex flint mines, similar flint mines also occurring in the Low Countries.

The Windmill Hill (also called Primary Neolithic) people rapidly spread from their initial area of colonisation, with one group reaching Scotland, variant types of Primary Neolithic bowls being found as far north as Aberdeenshire and even Sutherland. As yet however this pottery has not been found in Orkney, and so there is doubt as to whether the colonists reached the Northern Isles. By the time they reached Scotland, the Primary Neolithic communities seem to have lost most of the attributes of Windmill Hill—causewayed camps and flint mines are both confined to southern England—and evidence suggests that in Scotland they depended more on animal husbandry than on plant cultivation. Secondary Neolithic is the name given to this hybrid culture (see p 51).

In the Northern Isles

The first farmers who arrived in the Northern Isles, probably landing in Orkney early in the third millennium BC—we do not know the date for Shetland—found a more congenial climate than the modern visitor, with more abundant fauna and flora. Red deer abounded, and there was no shortage of wild fowl or fish. Although the northern winds had already denuded the islands of many trees, some still remained, a fact which is suggested by the variety of woods and woodworking tools from settlements like Skara Brae and Rinyo. Pollen samples found in the ditch of the chambered tomb of Maes Howe showed that at the time it was built (soon after 2500 BC) the surrounding countryside was predominantly heathland, but this was gradually taken over for pasture and there was a surprising increase in woodland. Pine seems to have persisted, supplemented by elm, oak and alder. No doubt the comparative freedom of Orkney from thick forest and peat bog made the islands particularly attractive to the early colonists, since there would have been little work in opening up farm land, an operation usually made difficult by the inadequacy of stone tools.

The character of the early pottery used by the Orcadian farmers is quite different from that of Windmill Hill. Most Orcadian pottery dates from the later second millennium BC and it must be supposed that the first settlers did not use pottery, perhaps using instead wooden or leather vessels. If they did it has not survived.

Collective tombs

The first farmers in Orkney are known from the impressive stone collective tombs which they built. These chambered tombs were more than just burial places, they represent in fact the surviving evidence for a religion or religions that affected much of western Europe from 3500 BC to 1500 BC—a period as long as that which has elapsed since the ministry of Christ. The tombs contained successive inhumations, probably of members of a single or related families, in much the same way that families were buried in a communal 'mort house' in seventeenth-century Scotland. But since complex religious ceremonies were performed at them, they may have sometimes served as temples as well.

As tombs are the main surviving monuments of the early farmers in western Europe, the question of their origins has long been the subject of debate among archaeologists, and the problems connected with them are far from being all solved. One of the difficulties lies in the fact that many different groups of chambered tombs are recognisable, some complex and some simple, and they are spread throughout Britain and Ireland, France, Spain and even Scandinavia. Most prehistorians now believe that they are indigenous developments of different regions, simple forms generally being the earliest. The characteristic feature of all the tombs (with the exception of those that are rock-cut) is that they employ large stones in their construction, for which reason they have been called 'megalithic' (ie 'big stone') monuments. This is a misleading term, since drystone walling was also employed in the building of the tombs, and sometimes they were constructed entirely of dry walling and corbelled roofs.

A key to the ancestry of the British chambered tombs is to be found in the series of unchambered long barrows (or burial mounds) associated with the earliest Windmill Hill communities in southern England. It is now known that there was a widespread custom of collective burial in early Neolithic England, bodies being collected together in rectilinear enclosures known as 'long mortuary enclosures' and sometimes housed in 'mortuary houses' where they were allowed to decay in the open air, protected from marauding animals, in much the same way that the dead are suspended from trees in wicker baskets in some parts of New Guinea today. When the bodies had decayed sufficiently a long trapezoidal mound was heaped up over the remains and structure to form an unchambered long barrow. These barrows are found outside the primary area of the Windmill Hill culture, and even occur sporadically along the east coast of Scotland, where one, at Daladies near Edzell in Angus, was recently excavated. There is a series in Yorkshire which appear to have had timber mortuary houses fired inside the barrow, such as Willerby Wold, the spaces left by the burning timbers forming draught channels. Similar mounds occur in western Britain and Ireland, where instead of earth mounds there are large stone tombs covered by cairns of stones. The relationship between these cairns and the long barrows is not clear, but they seem to be broadly contemporary and to have influenced one another. The origin of the unchambered long barrows is not known, though some archaeologists have seen the trapezoidal mound as being related to the trapezoidal houses of the Danube. Unfortunately, the only place where both houses and barrows occur is Poland, and here the barrows are of a different type and are unlikely to be earlier than the English ones such as the Wiltshire long barrow, Fussel's Lodge, which was built around 3200BC.

Some later megalithic tombs seem to be built on top of earlier timber structures. This phenomenon has been noted at Wayland's Smithy in Berkshire, where a chambered tomb was built on top of an earlier timber mortuary house. At Lochill, near Dumfries in Scotland, the first phase of construction was a rectangular timber structure with straight timber façade which were burned down and covered by a long cairn with a stone façade and a chamber without burials.

A further clue to the origin of megalithic chambered tombs is provided by multi-period tombs. In these, excavation has shown that two or more small stone tombs have been later incorporated into a larger mound. Where such primary megaliths occur they are usually simple, and are known as 'proto-megaliths'—they have been found in many parts of Britain, at Dyffryn Ardudwy in Wales, at Mid Gleniron in south-west Scotland, at Belas Knap in the Cotswolds and at Camster Long in Caithness. Current thinking favours the view that proto-megaliths are stone versions of mortuary houses and that long cairns, which are characteristically British, are derived from long barrows. One early type of megalith, known as a 'portal dolmen', found in Ireland and Wales (the earliest phase at Dyffryn was a portal dolmen), which consists of two portal stones at one end of a chamber forming an entrance and supporting a huge capstone, is possibly a translation of a timber structure for exposing corpses.

TYPES OF CHAMBERED TOMBS IN SCOTLAND (Fig 4)

There are several different groups of chambered tombs in Scotland, and in all about 360 examples have been recorded, of which over fifty are in Orkney and a similar number in Shetland (see p 36).

The earliest tombs are found round the mouth of the Clyde, particularly on Bute and Arran, and some are proto-megaliths; simple box-like chambers inspired possibly by timber prototypes from Yorkshire, and dating probably from before 3000 BC. They belong to a series widespread in the Irish Sea area, and were probably constructed sometime after the arrival of the first farmers.

These proto-megaliths developed second and sometimes third and

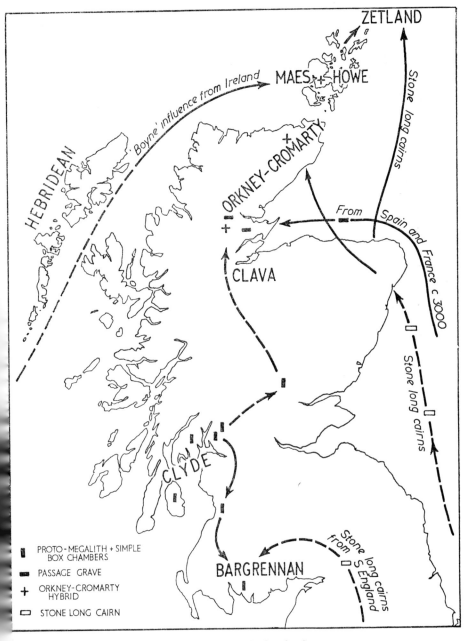

ZETLAND

Boyne influence from Ireland

MAES + HOWE

Stone long cairns

HEBRIDEAN

ORKNEY-CROMARTY

CLAVA

From   Spain and France c 3000

Stone long cairns

CLYDE

Stone long cairns

PROTO - MEGALITH + SIMPLE BOX CHAMBERS

PASSAGE GRAVE

+   ORKNEY-CROMARTY HYBRID

STONE LONG CAIRN

BARGRENNAN

Stone long cairns from S England

Fig 4   Possible spread of chambered tombs in Scotland

fourth chambers in front of the original chamber, portal stones being added to form a ritual entrance. At an early stage in their development the tombs with rectangular chambers seem to have spread fairly widely in western Scotland, and are found in Galloway, Ayrshire and Lanarkshire in the south, and even as far as Perthshire and possibly Easter Ross in the north.

Round the Clyde, later influence of the long trapezoidal mounds of Cotswold tombs resulted in the portal stones being incorporated into elaborate façades, with drystone walling, and these 'Clyde cairns' which probably evolved between 3000 and 2400 BC continued to be constructed until 2000 BC and later. Some Clyde cairns must have been in use a long time, for radiocarbon evidence from one, Monamore in Arran, dates the first phase to before 3000 BC and the final blocking of the chamber to around 2250 BC.

About 3000 BC a new type of chambered tomb appeared in Scotland, the passage grave, the earliest of which were composed of simple polygonal chambers with approach passages, set within a small cairn. They probably represent the arrival of people with origins in north-west France or the Iberian peninsula. Although the passage-grave builders had a limited influence in south-west Scotland, the new type of tomb was to have a greater effect in the north. In Easter Ross and east Sutherland the new passage-grave tradition became amalgamated with the already established tradition of rectangular chambers, and it is possible to recognise tombs both with polygonal bipartite chambers and with rectangular ones. Later developments led to tripartite tombs.

From this point onwards it is possible to recognise an 'Orkney-Cromarty' group of tombs in the area extending over the whole of Scotland north of the Beauly Firth. Within this province, due to considerable fusion of architectural traditions and local developments, can be found 'aberrant' varieties in the Hebrides, Caithness and the Northern Isles.

The Orkney-Cromarty chambered tombs (Fig 5)

The earliest types of Orkney-Cromarty tomb have not been recognised in the Northern Isles, but it is likely that Orkney was colonised by Neolithic farmers soon after Caithness, and it may well be that some early bipartite or tripartite tombs, ie tombs divided into sections, were built there soon after 3000 BC. Three Orkney tombs, Burgar, Cobbie Roo's Burden and Iphs, which have never been properly explored, may belong to this early period.

The early development of Orkney-Cromarty tombs was complicated by the arrival of two tomb features new in the Scottish north-east mainland. The first was the long cairn, the second was the heel-shaped cairn. The origin of the heel-shaped cairn is unknown, and the immediate ancestry of the long cairn uncertain, though it seems to be related to a class of Yorkshire monument at sites like Warter and Heslerton. The ultimate origin of both types may lie farther south still, in some as yet unrecognised class of timber mortuary enclosure. In a few Scottish mainland cases existing chambers seem to have been first incorporated in heel-shaped cairns, and subsequently further encased in a long cairn, the best example being one recently excavated at Tulach an t'Sionnach in Caithness. There, the heel cairn appears to have been added to an early type of passage grave, suggesting that in terms of sequence heel cairns were introduced at a time when passage graves of relatively early type were already established in north-east Scotland. Heel cairns are characteristic of the Scottish mainland; they do not occur in Orkney, but there is an important series in Shetland (see p 63). A few long cairns seem to have been adopted in Orkney, but in the main they are probably too early to have been fashionable in the main period of Orkney tomb building, which extends from around 2500 BC to possibly around 1650 BC.

There are thirty-six Orkney-Cromarty tombs in the Orkneys, of which six are in the guardianship of the Department of the Environment. They fall into three groups. The first is relatively rare, with a long passage ending in a chamber divided in three like Camster Round in Caithness; the most famous are Huntersquoy, Bigland Round and Sandyhill Smithy. They are the earliest in terms of development, though in terms of actual date they may not be much earlier than the

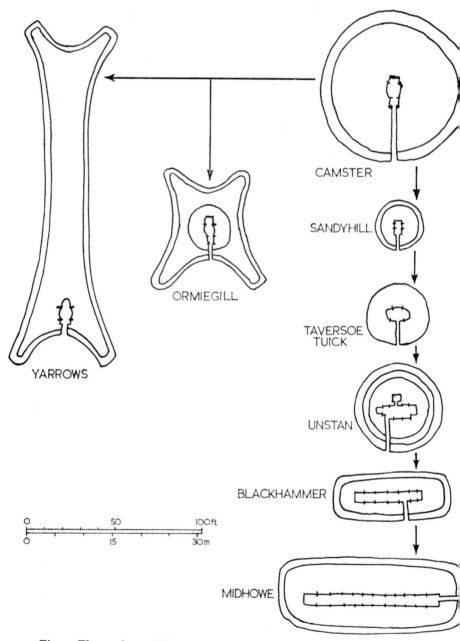

CAMSTER

SANDYHILL.

TAVERSOE
TUICK

UNSTAN

BLACKHAMMER

MIDHOWE

ORMIEGILL

YARROWS

0   50   100ft
0   15   30m

Fig 5   The typology of Orkney–Cromarty tombs (after Piggott)

other groups. Unlike the tombs of the Scottish mainland they have the Orcadian features of stone benches or shelves between the partition stones. They are 'tripartite chamber tombs'.

The second group is the most distinctive. These tombs are known as 'stalled cairns', and are derived from the tripartite chambered tombs. In this group the burial chamber was gradually enlarged by the addition of compartments until the tombs became very long and quite unlike Camster-type passage graves. The process started in Caithness, but it is in Orkney that the really bizarre variants occur. The earliest in the sequence are in small round cairns, but as they develop they are enclosed by long cairns.

The last group is known as the 'Bookan type', after a site near Stenness on Mainland, dug last century and now only a grassy mound (Fig 6). There are only three tombs in this group, Calf of Eday North-West, Calf of Eday South-East, and Bookan, though the lower chamber in Taversoe Tuick and Huntersquoy are closely related, as is the mini-subterranean chamber at Taversoe Tuick. The chambers are roughly oval in these tombs, divided into four compartments with the exception of Bookan, which is divided into five.

Rituals performed. It would appear from the excavated tombs that the bodies were laid in a crouched position in the compartments formed by the divisional slabs, with their heads in the angles. Sometimes they were laid on the stone benches or shelves, if these existed. When later burials were laid in the tombs it seems that the earlier bodies, now reduced to skeletons, were pushed aside or gathered up in one part of the chamber, care being taken to preserve the skulls, which were sometimes set upright. Other bones seem to have mattered less, and were sometimes lost. Up to twenty or thirty bodies were laid in a single tomb.

When the burials were in place, grave goods were laid in the chamber, usually pots, sometimes accompanied by flints. The pots with a couple of exceptions have always been found shattered, and are usually incomplete. This suggests that they were deliberately broken,

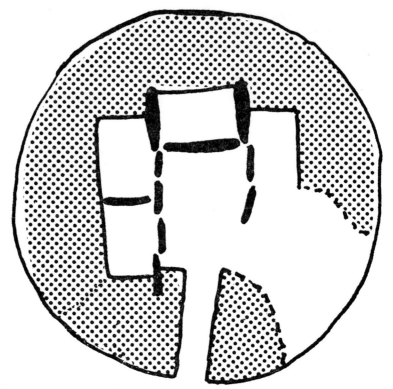

Fig 6   Bookan—plan of chambered tomb (after Drylen)

either at the tomb itself or perhaps elsewhere. This act might have
been to release the 'spirit 'of the vessel so that it might pass with the
dead to the next world, as some contemporary primitive societies
believe. Fragments may have been removed after breaking for ritual
reasons, and indeed the custom of taking small bones from skeletons
already in the tombs might help to explain why skeletons are so often
incomplete. The pots were not new vessels made for burial, but had
already seen domestic service. Often the pottery was laid in a heap
apart from the burials, sometimes in hollows made in the floor of the

chambers. At Unstan such a hollow was made in the clay floor, containing several sherds of different pots.

Fire seems to have had an important part to play in the rituals carried out and chamber floor, bones and finds not infrequently show traces of burning. In the Knowe of Yarso on Rousay fires had been lit in the chamber, and both sides of all compartments were reddened and cracked, with traces of soot, and ash and charred wood were detected on the floor. In some cases fire had raged through most of the chamber, in others it was localised. Sometimes the burials were scorched, but occasionally later burials were made after the fire ceremony, and skeletons have been found above a layer of ash. In some tombs, including Midhowe and Taversoe Tuick, there was no trace of fire at all. Although it appears that the pots in the tombs were broken before burning, this does not mean that the burning of the pots was an integral part of the ritual, it was probably accidental.

Animal bones have occasionally been found in large quantities. The Rousay cairns have two deposits of animal bones, the first contemporary with the use of the tomb, the second associated with the ritual blocking. The bones for the most part belong to edible animals, suggesting funerary feasts or offerings of food. There are dog remains from several tombs, possibly offerings connected with hunting ceremonies. The abundant remains of deer in the burial deposits prove that the users were hunters as well as farmers. Calf of Eday Long and Sandyhill Smithy produced otter bones.

Usually the last act was the blocking of the tomb, the passage and chamber being sometimes filled with earth and stones. At Blackhammer and Knowe of Yarso burials were made after the filling of the chamber or at least the inner part of the passage had been completed. It is possible that these were 'guardians' of the tomb.

Outside a few tombs there has been found slight evidence for other rituals. Two tripartite tombs on Rousay had hollows outside the entrance, in one case filled with ashes, bone, flint and pottery. At Isbister there was a cache of objects outside the inner wall face of the tomb.

Maes Howe tombs (Fig 7; Pls 1–2)

The second main class of chambered tomb in Orkney is named after the prototype at Maes Howe, at the south-west end of Loch Harray on Mainland.

There are ten cairns which belong to this class, all confined to the Orkneys. Six are on Mainland, in an almost straight line bisecting the island from east to west. Two further cairns are on Eday, and one each on Sanday and the Holm of Papa Westray.

The earliest tombs are to be found only on Mainland and Eday; they consist, apart from Maes Howe, of Cuween Hill, Wideford Hill, (Pl 2a) and Vinquoy Hill (Eday). The destroyed cairn known as the Ring of Bookan is also probably early, the surviving ditch round it being similar to that at Maes Howe itself.

The first of the later tombs is also to be found on Mainland, at Quanterness. The remainder consist of Quoyness (Sanday), Eday Manse (Eday) and the Holm of Papa Westray.

The characteristic feature of the Maes Howe tombs is a square or rectangular chamber approached by a passage. From the main chamber small openings lead into a number of cells, more or less symmetrically arranged. The roof of the main chamber is high, angular and corbelled. The roofs are usually unnecessarily high, Maes Howe rising 15ft above floor level, Quoyness 13ft and even the smaller tombs of Wideford and Cuween at least 8ft and 7½ft. The building in all the tombs is remarkably good, and at Maes Howe outstanding. From Maes Howe there are two lines of development, one towards smaller chambers with less symmetrical plans, the other towards an increase of size and number of chambers.

The inspiration behind the appearance of the Maes Howe tombs must have been the arrival in Orkney of newcomers from Ireland. There, on the Boyne, are a series of passage graves, of which the finest and most famous is Newgrange in County Meath. There are striking similarities between Newgrange and Maes Howe, and from this it has been inferred that Maes Howe was built around 2500 BC as this is the date assigned to Newgrange by the radiocarbon method.

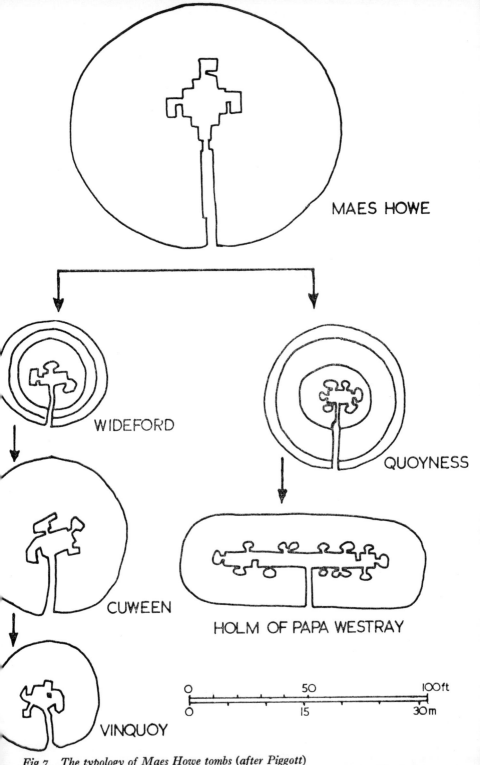

MAES HOWE

WIDEFORD

QUOYNESS

CUWEEN

HOLM OF PAPA WESTRAY

VINQUOY

| 0 | 50 | 100ft |
| 0 | 15 | 30m |

Fig 7   *The typology of Maes Howe tombs (after Piggott)*

At this period both Bookan-type and tripartite stalled cairns were being built in Orkney, one tripartite stalled tomb, that at Knowe of Lairo on Rousay, being converted around 2400 BC or slightly later to a Maes Howe type of tomb. During the latter part of the third millennium both Maes Howe tombs and stalled cairns continued to develop, the very devolved tombs of the Holm of Papa Westray and the Knowe of Ramsay carrying the sequence down to the eighteenth century BC.

Apart from the tomb type, there is little to connect Orkney with the Valley of the Boyne, though certain types of objects, notably large bone pins and macehead pendants, do point to other connections between the two areas.

Maes Howe (Fig 8). Maes Howe is probably the finest example of prehistoric architecture in north-west Europe. The present mound, made up of clay and stones, is about 24ft high and 115ft in diameter. It stands on a platform, surrounded by a broad flat-bottomed ditch. Within the mound lies the tomb itself, approached by a passage 31ft long. When the tomb was built, against the centre base of the wall face of the chamber, a layer of peats was deposited, overlaid with clay. Within the mound two rough revetment walls were constructed, 11ft apart and about 2½ft high, with a pronounced inward batter, which seem to have been built to consolidate the sloping layers of the mound during its construction. The core of the mound round the chamber consists of rubble faced by a carefully built wall constructed in a series of steps, standing to a height of over 14ft above a plinth. When the whole mound was completed, a palisade was set in a trench round the perimeter of the mound.

The construction of the stone chamber and approach passage are however the most remarkable feature of the monument. Orcadian sandstone splits easily along the bedding plane, which makes the cutting of building stone relatively easy. The builders of Maes Howe however not only used small slabs of sandstone but also large blocks (the largest of which weighs over 3 tons), which in some cases were carefully dressed. These huge blocks have been carefully adjusted,

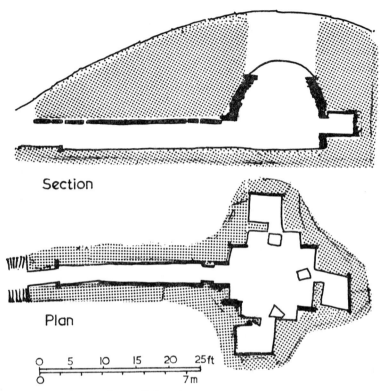

Section

Plan

0   5   10   15   20   25ft

0   7 m

Fig 8   Maes Howe—plan and elevation

small slivers of sandstone being used as underpinnings in places, while others have been carefully rebated to take the corner of an adjoining block exactly. Some joints are so minutely adjusted that it is not possible to pass the blade of a knife between them. No mortar of any kind was used in the building, and much of the dressing of the stones was done with hammers and stone mauls. The walls of the main chamber rise up vertically to a height of about $4\frac{1}{2}$ft, after which they converge gently to a height of about $8\frac{1}{2}$ft, the natural oblique fracture of the stone being used to give a smooth face to the wall. The upper part uses oversailing blocks to form a square corbelled vault. In the

45

corners of the central chamber, which is 15ft square, buttresses support the roof where it is most required.

Three smaller chambers open off the main chamber, and were once closed by large blocks which now lie on the floor of the central chamber. The approach passage too seems to have been blocked by a large stone which could slide into a recess in the passage wall. The passage was possibly an open trench for the first 22½ft, thereafter there is a step down and it runs inside the mound, roofed with slabs. It is about 4½ft high.

The tomb was opened in 1861, but it was found to have been plundered previously. On several occasions in the twelfth century parties of Norse had entered the tomb, leaving behind them a series of twenty-four runic inscriptions, the second largest collection from any one site (the largest collection coming from Bergen). These inscriptions, the kind that might be expected about the charms of particular Norse ladies, and a series of proper names, record how the Norse Crusaders broke into the howe to shelter from a storm, and one of the party went mad. Several inscriptions refer to treasure, for example 'Hakon single-handed bore treasure from this howe'. It was common in Norse tradition to believe that howes or burial mounds contained treasure, frequently guarded by protecting monsters. Very possibly the tomb did contain gold, for gold 'sun discs' were found in one of the Knowes of Trotty, dating from the early Bronze Age.

The construction techniques found in Maes Howe are also encountered in other tombs of the same group, though not as well developed. The device of using a stepped wall occurs for example at Quoyness, where there are two concentric wall faces and two subsidiary walls within the cairn.

Burial rites. Very little is known about the burial rites associated with the Maes Howe type of tomb. Burials were not laid neatly in the cells leading from the main chamber; both chamber and passage were used as well, and the skeletons left disarticulated, except in one instance at Quanterness. At Cuween a skull was carefully set in a recess in a cell

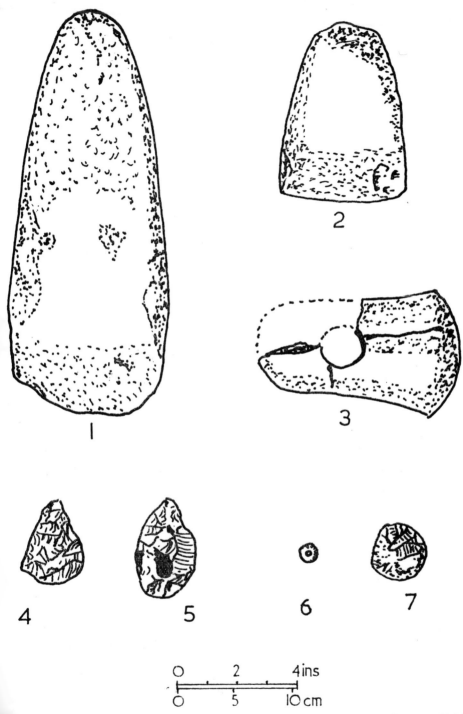

1

2

3

4   5   6   7

O ⊢━━━━ 2 ━━━━ 4ins
O ⊢━━━━ 5 ━━━━ 10cm

9   *Typical objects of Unstan culture 1, 2, 4, 5 Calf of Eoay Long 3, 6, 7 Taversoe Tuick*

wall. At Quoyness long bones were laid in a circular stone cist in the chamber, protected by a coverstone.

The only evidence for burning was at Cuween, where some bones 'showed evidence of cremation'. The presence of a recess at the entrance of Maes Howe into which the door blocking stone could slide suggests that the tombs were re-opened for successive burials. Quoyness, Cuween and Wideford Hill all had deliberately blocked passages, and other tombs also had blocked chambers. Maes Howe was never filled in.

Bones, sherds and ash found at Quoyness have been interpreted as the remains of a ritual meal consumed on top of the cairn. There is however a dearth of grave goods in Maes Howe tombs, and this might be a feature of the associated rituals, though could be the result of robbing. Only Quoyness has produced relics.

The Dwarfie Stane—a rock-cut tomb (Fig 1)

There is a single, famous example of a chambered tomb in Orkney that is not built but hewn out of a huge free-standing erratic block. This is the Dwarfie Stane on Hoy. It resembles a Mediterranean rock-cut tomb, though these were cut from the living rock not boulders. With the exception of a possible rock-cut tomb at Glendalough (Wicklow), the nearest parallels are in Iberia and on the Marne. Tempting though it is to regard it as a direct result of contact with the Mediterranean, it is more probably a purely local product, the plan being that of a variant of the Bookan type of tomb. The lower chamber at Taversoe Tuick is also rock-cut in part.

CHAMBERED-TOMB BUILDING CULTURES (Figs 9–10)

The builders of the chambered tombs would appear to be two different groups, to some extent contemporary. The Orkney-Cromarty tombs were built by a group of people belonging to the Unstan culture. Their characteristic pottery is best represented at the stalled cairn of Unstan on Mainland. The dearth of finds from the Maes Howe type tombs leaves the identity of the builders uncertain, but they appear to have

1a   Maes Howe chambered tomb, exterior, Orkney

1b   Maes Howe chambered tomb, interior, Orkney

2a Wideford Hill chambered tomb, showing concentric walling, Orkney
2b The entrance to the Knowe of Lairo chambered tomb, Rousay, Orkney

had contacts with the builders of villages like Skara Brae and Rinyo—
the Grooved Ware people.

The Unstan culture

It would appear that at first the Neolithic settlers in Britain remained aloof from the native food-gathering communities which they
found already in these islands. These native peoples were conservative,
and at first made no attempt to give up their old ways and adopt new
ideas such as farming and the manufacture of pottery. Gradually however they adopted various ideas from the invaders, and modified them
to their own needs. These hybrid communities are known as Secondary
Neolithic cultures. The Secondary Neolithic people of Scotland with
certain exceptions seem to have had their origins in England, whence
they arrived with their distinctive decorated pottery, transverse arrowheads, flint knives with polished edges and jet 'belt fasteners'. In
Scotland, the cultures underwent further modification, and further
distinctive types of pottery evolved without parallel south of the
Solway-Tyne.

Pottery akin to the earliest wares from Windmill Hill and Hembury
seems to have spread from Yorkshire to south and east Scotland around
the beginning of the third millennium BC. Sometime before 2500 BC
plain and lugged bowls appear in western Scotland, derived from
Wessex, whence also came angled shoulders and linear decorated
pottery. These new styles soon spread throughout the country, and
towards 2000 BC new impetus from Ireland resulted in new styles of
pottery evolving in west-central Scotland. These spread to the
Hebrides and Orkney, and it is not quite certain whether the Unstan
forms of pottery, which are one of the products of this tradition,
originated in the Hebrides or in Orkney itself. Unstan-style pots have
also been found in Caithness (at a tomb called Kenny's Cairn) and in
Sutherland (at a tomb near Lairg). Unstan pottery consists of two
classes of vessels—plain round-bottomed bowls, and shallow open
bowls with vertical collars usually more elaborately decorated in
channelled or 'stab-and-drag' technique.

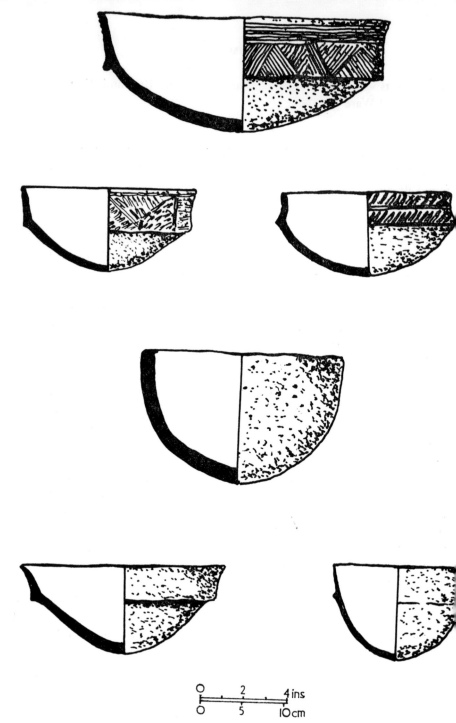

Fig 10   *Neolithic pottery of Unstan type from Taversoe Tuick, Orkney*

Although certain associated objects like leaf-shaped arrowheads are characteristic of Windmill Hill farmers, evidence suggests that the Orkney tomb builders encountered already existing Secondary Neolithic cultures on the Scottish mainland, from whom they acquired certain types of objects. Stone maceheads, of which one example was found in Unstan itself, are characteristic of Secondary Neolithic people in Yorkshire and Derbyshire, as are polished flint knives and transverse arrowheads of the type found at Unstan.

The Unstan farmers grew barley and domesticated the ox, sheep, goat and pig. They hunted deer, horse and sea birds, and caught fish. Nothing is known of their houses, which were probably of turf, and their settlements are only indicated by occasional scatters of flints and

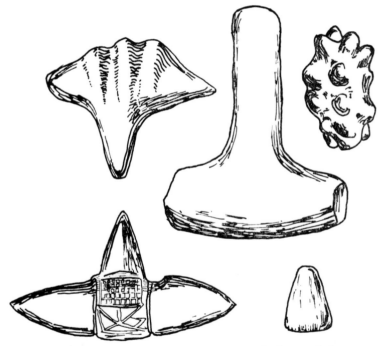

Fig 11   Rinyo-Clacton stone objects (after Piggott). Scale: nearly ½

pottery, notably along the slopes of Wideford Hill. They were probably sub-rectangular or oval, and scattered rather than clustered in villages.

Skara Brae and the Rinyo culture (Figs 11–13)

The second group of Neolithic people in Orkney seem to have come to the islands after the Orkney-Cromarty farming tomb builders and followed a rather different way of life, more akin to their food-gathering predecessors, food production being apparently on a limited scale. These people are known from two remarkable village sites, at Skara Brae on Mainland and Rinyo on Rousay, and are generally known as Grooved Ware people (or sometimes Rinyo-Clacton) on account of their decorated pottery (Fig 13).

The Grooved Ware people were pastoralists who bred sheep and cattle. Until further excavations were carried out at Skara Brae in 1972, they were believed not to have grown grain, but now there are seed grains from a midden there which may indicate that barley was grown. They supplemented their diet with shell-fish, notably limpets. Their material equipment was very simple: polished stone axes and adzes, rough stone knives and an assortment of bone utensils including shovels. Whale vertebrae were used as paint pots and bowls, and pendants were made from walrus ivory. Beads were devised from bones or teeth, and bones were also used to make decorative pins. They also made rather mysterious decorated stone balls, the function of which is unknown (could they have been used in a game?), and equally mysterious spiked stone 'maces' which have parallels from the taiga zone of North Eurasia.

Their pottery was coarse, but elaborately decorated with grooving or applied strips and blobs. Its origins are obscure, and have been the subject of considerable debate. Grooved ware is found fairly widespread in Britain, being associated with many important Neolithic sites in Wessex, such as at the henge monuments of Durrington Walls, Woodhenge or even the first phase of Stonehenge itself. Many different groups or styles of grooved ware are known, and the distribution ex-

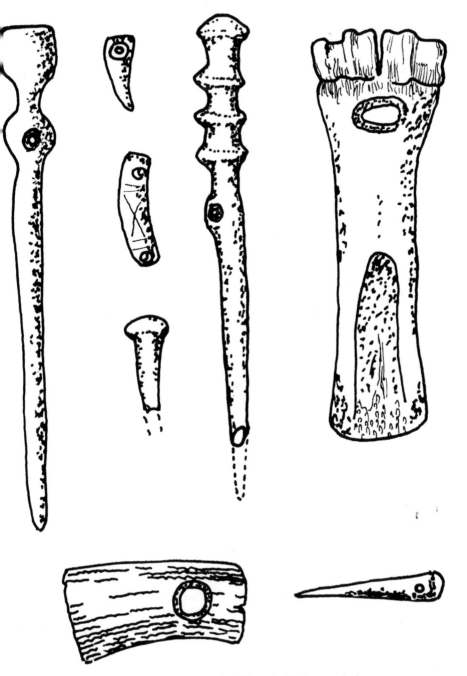

Fig 12   *Rinyo-Clacton bone objects (after Piggott). Scale: nearly* ½

tends up to Yorkshire and the Pennines. In Scotland, apart from a few finds from the south-west, there seems to be a general dearth of sites outside Orkney. Whether the Orkney grooved ware culture is connected with the English groups is difficult to determine, though it seems possible that there was a connection between Yorkshire and Orkney at least. Certainly this type of pottery, with elaborate grooved or plastic ornament, seems to be a peculiar manifestation of the Secondary Neolithic cultures of Britain, and may be no more than an endeavour, by the native substratum in Britain, to represent basketry in pottery forms. In England the general cultural attributes differ markedly from those in Orkney, with certain exceptions.

Grooved ware may go back to the Middle Neolithic (c 2500 BC)—certainly it was in use c 2000 BC as recent radiocarbon dates from Durrington Walls have shown—and if the association of a Beaker from the last phase at Rinyo can be accepted (and there are also possible Beaker sherds from an early level at Skara Brae), it must have continued in use at least in Orkney until c 1650 BC.

Connections between the two cultures

The relationship between the Orkney-Cromarty tomb builders and the Grooved Ware people can be demonstrated in a number of ways. Pottery of the same fabric as Unstan ware was found in the earliest layers at Rinyo, and certain objects of Rinyo type (notably maceheads) have been found associated with Orkney-Cromarty tombs. The stronger link between chambered-tomb builders and the Grooved Ware people is seen however in the Maes Howe tombs. Spiked stone objects and a bone pin from Quoyness are Rinyo types, as is the face motif on Skara Brae pottery that appears again in a slightly different version at the Holm of Papa Westray.

It is difficult to believe that the Grooved Ware people were responsible for the building of tombs like Maes Howe, and indeed the only known burial definitely associated with them in Orkney was of a woman buried under the wall of one of the houses at Skara Brae, in quite a different manner from that customary in the area. It is possible the

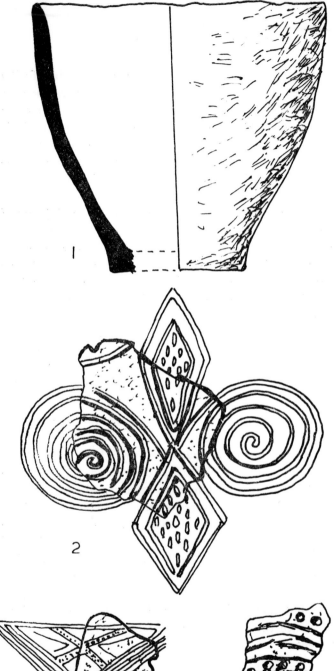

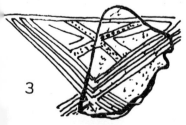

Fig 13 Grooved ware
1 Plain pot from
Rinyo. Scale:
approx ¼
2–4 Decorated sherds
from Skara Brae and
Rinyo (decor restored).
Scale: slightly under ½

tombs of Maes Howe type were built by other people but finally blocked by Grooved Ware pastoralists. A parallel instance can be seen at West Kennet in Wiltshire, where a chambered tomb built by one culture was finally blocked by another some centuries later. The finds from Quoyness may have been brought there with the material used to block the tomb. Another theory, though improbable, is that the Grooved Ware people built the Maes Howe tombs for some outside overlord.

Certain designs on pottery from Skara Brae are very reminiscent of designs found in chambered tombs on the Boyne, the most notable example being a sherd with a double spiral and double-lozenge pattern from Skara Brae. These abstract designs are seen reflected in the Boyne tombs of Newgrange and Knowth. It seems virtually certain that there was some connection between the people of the Boyne and Orkney, but the precise nature of that contact remains unknown.

Summary (Fig 14)

The first settlers in Orkney were farmers who brought with them from the mainland of Scotland the Orkney-Cromarty tombs, which were built over a period of many centuries. We know little about the material possessions of the first settlers, but later they can be distinguished as the Unstan culture.

At a late stage in the history of chambered-tomb building the Maes Howe type of tomb appeared in Orkney, centred on Mainland; the earlier Orkney-Cromarty tombs tended to be scattered over the more remote islands. The people who were responsible for the Maes Howe tombs had some connection with the Unstan people (possibly actually taking over the Orkney-Cromarty tomb of the Knowe of Lairo and converting it to a Maes Howe type), and with the Grooved Ware pastoralists who had now settled in Orkney. There also seems to have been some direct contact between the Grooved Ware people and the Unstan culture, but only at an early stage in the development of the Rinyo culture, since the Unstan type of fabric only appears in the earliest settlement.

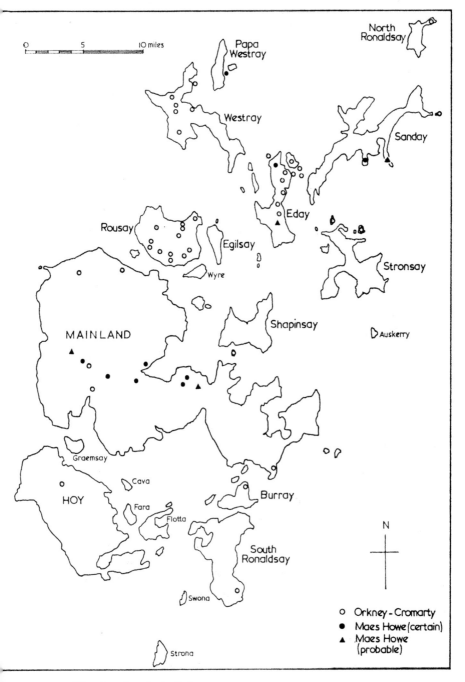

Fig 14 *Chambered tombs in Orkney*

THE VILLAGES OF SKARA BRAE AND RINYO (Fig 15; Pl 4a)
The village sites of Skara Brae on Mainland and Rinyo on Rousay are
unique in northern Europe, for they preserve in stone their original
furnishings. It must not be thought that the internal arrangements of
the houses were unique to Orkney, but that owing to the peculiar
character of the Orkney standstone and lack of wood, stone was used
to make furnishings that elsewhere would have been made of timber
and would have perished. This use of stone is a recurring feature in
Orkney, and one can see slab-built cupboards in some of the post-
medieval Orcadian farmhouses.

Of the two sites, Skara Brae is the best preserved, situated on the
beach at Skaill Bay. It was first exposed in a storm in 1850, when a
midden and some huts were laid open. The Laird of Skaill carried out
some excavation, and by 1868 four huts had been cleared. Apart from
desultory digging, nothing further was done on the site till 1925, when
a storm stripped and removed part of the midden and revealed more
structures. From 1927 to 1930, Gordon Childe, who was then professor
of archaeology at Edinburgh, carried out excavations on the site in

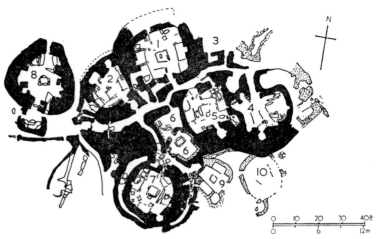

Fig 15 Skara Brae—plan (after Childe). The numbers indicate houses

advance of consolidation. The settlement was so remarkably well preserved that even Childe was unconvinced of its antiquity, and believed that grooved ware was a local variant of Bronze Age incrusted urn pottery and suggested an upper date limit of 500 BC. The excavation report indeed was published in 1931 under the misleading title *Skara Brae, a Pictish Village in Orkney*. Curiously only a few years later Walter Grant began excavating at Rinyo, and found a Beaker sherd. Childe was called in to complete the excavation, and it was found that although only the lowest courses were preserved, unlike the Skara Brae village, the settlements were nevertheless almost identical and that Rinyo came to an end in the Beaker period, c 1650 BC.

At both Skara Brae and Rinyo there were several periods of rebuilding, but the overall character of the villages remained similar throughout their occupation. The standard house type is a square with rounded corners, measuring about 15ft to 20ft across, entered by a single doorway, which had in some instances elaborate bar-holes and sometimes an intra-mural cell behind. In the centre of each house a peat fire was burned on a stone hearth. Against the back wall of the house stood a dresser, and during excavations at least one pot was found in place on it. On either side of the hearth were fixed beds formed of three slabs to keep off draughts and to retain the bedding, presumably of skins. Over this would have been a skin canopy supported by stone posts. The bed on the right-hand side of the door on entering was larger than that on the left, and on the evidence of recent Hebridean custom it may be inferred that the right-hand bed was for the husband and the left-hand one for his wife. Above each bed was a shelf for possessions. Boxes were set in the floor and lined with clay. These presumably stored some liquid, and it may be that they were filled with water in order to keep shellfish alive.

One house lay outside the settlement and had a central hearth but no beds nor dresser. This was possibly a workshop, where a potter or maker of stone tools worked. It could have been the workshop of one man who supplied the village with pots and tools, or a communal workshop. It is just possible that it might have served as a byre. At

Rinyo, more than one hut had clay ovens built on a stone slab beside the hearth.

The walls of the houses were corbelled upwards for about 8 or 10ft, and then were roofed possibly with whalebone or driftwood rafters supporting turf or thin slabs of stone. They do not appear to have had completely corbelled roofs. Wood may have been driftwood, but could also have been found locally. Alder and hazel twigs were found at Skara Brae, and alder, birch, willow, pine and oak at Rinyo, where there were also holes for timber posts.

In its final form Skara Brae, after several phases of rebuilding, consisted of six houses, leading off a covered alley. In this last phase the whole settlement was covered with a midden of ash, dung and broken bones which even filled the spaces between the houses and was heaped up over them to a height of 8ft, only the roofs protruding. It was kept from collapse by a drystone retaining wall, rather like those used in chambered tombs to retain the cairn. Unsavoury though this may have been, it did serve to keep out the cold northern winter winds. It would be erroneous to think that the Skara Brae people lived in a state of total squalor; individual drains led from the houses to a substantial stone sewer.

The excavation of 1972, run jointly by the National Museum of Antiquities in Edinburgh and Edinburgh University, was confined to examining the midden to find out more about the economy of the people. The abundant mammal, bird, fish and rodent bones have, at the time of writing, not yet been examined, and only a small sample of the organic material; but it appears that the plant life round the settlement consisted of moss, sedge, grass, dandelion, campion and plantain, the last of particular interest since it is a weed of cultivation. The other botanical specimens imply a similar sort of plant cover to that which exists at present. The excavation produced similar finds to those from the previous excavations, but included a hitherto unknown type of tool and decorated stones, one with traces of ochre infilling in part of the design. Carvings adorn the passage walls in the village; other inscribed stones were found previously.

NEOLITHIC SHETLAND

Although the origins of the first farming communities in Shetland are unknown, their peoples were responsible for the building of a remarkable series of settlements and chambered tombs that are absolutely without close parallel. These Shetland monuments, taken together, provide a unique picture of life and death in early prehistoric Shetland. Almost as many chambered tombs are known in these islands as in Orkney, and no doubt many more remain to be recorded. Fifty-seven have so far been noted, most of them in a very ruined condition.

The Shetland monuments are strikingly different from the Orkney tombs. The majority belong to what is known as the Zetland group, and have trefoil-shaped or rectangular chambers constructed of large irregular blocks of stone which, though difficult to build with, have been utilised with great skill by the builders. The cairns enclosing them tend to be small, one, Sobul, measuring only 14ft by 11ft. The chambers are approached by narrow passages, between 2 and 4ft wide, and from about 4½ to 13ft long. Some cairns are round, while six are square, edged with walling and with traces of a façade in three cases.

The Shetland heel cairns (Fig 16)

By far the majority of the cairns in the Zetland group are heel-shaped in plan, and for that reason are known as the Shetland heel cairns. They are faced with a curving façade, from the centre of which the passage runs back to the chamber. These façades are carefully built, almost always with tall upright stones to finish off the ends.

Of the heel cairns, the best preserved is Vementry, off the west of Mainland. Here there is a circular cairn 26ft in diameter with a chamber, round which is a heel-shaped platform. Probably the cairn originally formed a low dome. A curious feature of Vementry is the fact that its façade is unbroken for an entrance. Access was gained by a drop from behind the façade into the passage, which was possibly open until it joined the cairn facing-wall. It would seem that the lower courses of chamber and passage were built first; then the chamber, passage and cairn were completed; and finally the front of

63

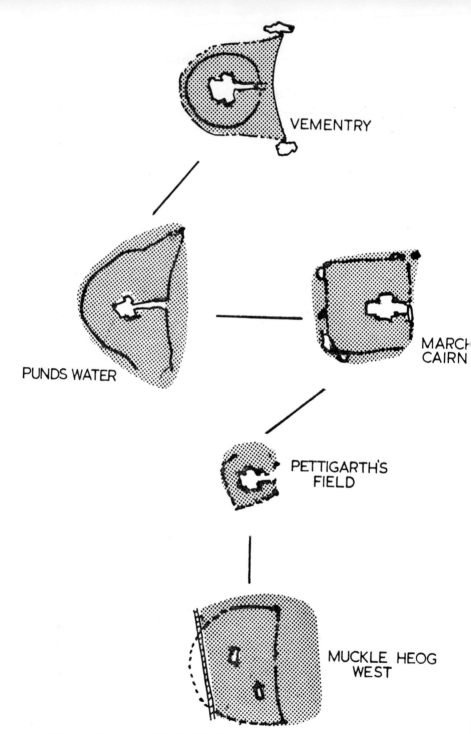

VEMENTRY

PUNDS WATER

MARCH CAIRN

PETTIGARTH'S FIELD

MUCKLE HEOG WEST

Fig 16   Typology of Shetland heel cairns

the platform filled in behind the façade. Other heel cairns also seem to have had no break in the façade for the entrance passage, and indeed at one monument, the Beorgs of Uyea, passage and chamber are both subterranean, the passage mouth being built up against a rock face so there must have been a drop down into the passage.

A few cairns seem to have had no passage or chamber, their place being taken by stone cists, the best example of this being the Muckle Heog West. The cists there are about the same size as those of the Bronze Age.

The cairns were all probably fairly low; the roof level of the chambers at Vementry and Ronas Hill was only about 6ft and 4ft above ground.

Vementry and other sites suggest that the Shetland heel cairns known today represent the combination of two separate elements, a heel-shaped cairn and a passage grave. It seems probable that the heel-shaped cairn was introduced to Shetland at a much earlier date than the passage grave, though no example of an early heel cairn has yet been recognised in the islands. They are known to be early however because similar cairns have been found elsewhere, most notably at Tullach an t'Sionnaich in Caithness, where a heel cairn was incorporated into a later long cairn (p 37). Long cairns are absent from Shetland.

An overall study of the existing Shetland cairns suggests a series of developments from narrow heel-shaped cairns into wide cairns with elaborate façades which in turn develop into square cairns. The earliest are almost certainly round cairns built on top of a platform with a façade, like Vementry.

The development of the plan of the chambers to some extent supports this theory of development. It would seem that the earliest have trefoil chambers, while later the rectangular chambers become more common and finally there is a fusion with the Shetland tradition of Bronze Age burial in stone cists, when the cists are themselves incorporated into the cairns. The drop into the entrance at Vementry might be seen as the result of the fusion of the traditions of passage grave and heel cairn; where the entry to the passage penetrates the façade it is probably fairly late in such a building sequence.

Apart from the Shetland heel cairns there is another small group of tombs in Shetland, the round passage graves. These are very few in number and very ruined, and the only thing that can really be said of them is that they are not ancestral to the Shetland heel cairns.

Rituals. A number of the Shetland cairns seem to be oriented to the south-east. Very little information however is obtainable about the burial rites, since no bones were found in any of the cairns excavated this century, and earlier accounts are confusing. There is some evidence that the forecourts were blocked, and indeed at one cairn the blocking was even edged with a length of walling imitating the façade itself. There is no evidence however for rituals taking place in the forecourts, and the general tendency for the latter to flatten out suggests that they were not in fact used for ritual observances.

In the same way there is very little evidence from scientifically excavated cairns for the material culture of the builders. A lost sherd with string decoration from a tomb called Giant's Grave may have been a piece of Beaker, but this site and the only other to have produced pottery, Pettigarths Field, was dug before the days of recording in detail and nothing is known for certain of the character of the sherds. In this connection it is worth noting that a Beaker sherd was found at the so-called Stanydale Temple.

Steatite vessels were found in a cist in the Muckle Heog East cairn. Three were small and square, similar to one found in a Bronze Age oval house at Jarlshof. The Muckle Heog vessels were reportedly found with a skull, and could have been primary, the tomb being typologically late in the Shetland series.

The Shetland cairns seem to have been sited on prominent locations, preferably hills, and are often in areas remote from more recent habitation. They are however often near settlement sites, and the character of houses in Neolithic Shetland is so similar to the cairns that they must be considered in the same context.

3a   Bigland Round, chambered tomb, Rousay, Orkney
3b   Stanydale 'Temple', Shetland

4a Skara Brae, Orkney, interior of house showing stone furnishings
4b Bronze Age village, Jarlshof, Shetland

'Temples' and houses (Figs 17–18; Pl 3b)

The Neolithic house sites of Shetland are characterised by having an approximately oval plan, the main chamber having one or two side cells or recesses, recalling the compartments of a chambered tomb. They are stone built, and have in common with the chambered tombs skilfully constructed masonry which manages to utilise large and amorphous blocks of stone without loss of stability in the structure. Similarly, the portals and ends of the cell divisions are constructed with upright monoliths as in the Shetland tombs.

The later Shetland tombs seem to span the period from about 2000 to 1500 BC. This date bracket seems reasonable for the earliest of the

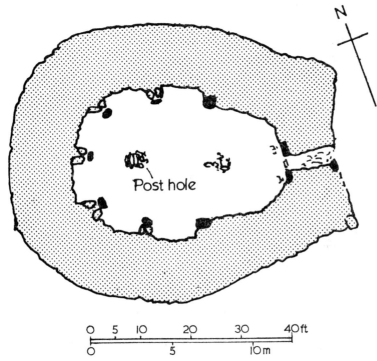

Fig 17   Stanydale 'Temple' plan (after Calder)

Shetland house sites, but these continued to be built until the arrival of metalworkers at the end of the Bronze Age brought to an end the Shetland Stone Age.

A curious type of monument which links the tombs with the humbler dwellings are the sites described by their excavator, C. S. T. Calder, as 'temples'. The most famous is Stanydale on Shetland Mainland, which is situated among smaller but similar houses and their associated fields. The Stanydale temple is much larger than any Shetland heel cairn. Its large chamber is big enough to accommodate one, and measures 39ft by 22ft. Unlike many of the house sites it is however heel-shaped, and in keeping with most tombs is oriented south-east. Within the chamber were two post-holes containing the remains of spruce posts, and further remains of spruce and pine were found on the floor and interpreted by the excavator as being from the roof. Spruce is not found in Scotland except as a deliberate introduction in recent times, and the most probable source for the wood in the Stanydale site is America, from which it could have drifted. It is also possible, but much less likely, that it was brought deliberately from Norway. It is hardly likely that the entire area occupied by the Stanydale temple was roofed with timber; the walls are not substantial enough to carry such a roof especially in the absence of all but two roof supports, and there was a local shortage of timber. It is of course possible that the posts were not intended to support any kind of roof, but were of the nature of totem poles.

Two related sites are situated on Whalsay, and are known as the Benie Hoose (or Bunyie Hoose) and the Standing Stones of Yoxie. When they were excavated it was believed that the Benie Hoose was a habitation site, possibly occupied by the 'priests' who officiated in the 'temple' about 100yd away. Both Yoxie and the Benie Hoose differ from Stanydale in that they have horned forecourts, giving them a figure-of-eight profile. Yoxie, like Stanydale, is a substantial structure, about 61ft long by 36ft wide, while the Benie Hoose is even larger, about 80ft long. The Benie Hoose has recessed cells in the forecourt and is furnished with drains. Both structures showed signs of con-

inuing use or re-use at a later period, and some of the finds from
Yoxie are Iron Age in character. On account of the general absence of
occupation material from Yoxie, with the exception of 120–30 crude
stone implements including hammer and anvil stones, it was felt that
it was never regularly inhabited in the Neolithic. In contrast, apart
from drains there was abundant evidence of occupation at the Benie
Hoose, including thirty-three broken or complete trough querns, and
1,800 stone implements—hammer stones and pounders, axes, picks,
pot lids, a steatite pot handle and a flat steatite spindle whorl were
among them. There were also considerable numbers of pot sherds.
Small steatite plugs may have been used for skin floats in fishing.

Attempts have been made to see parallels between the Shetland
temples and those of prehistoric Malta, and it must be admitted that
there are strong similarities. It would be unwise however to suggest
that there is any connection between them, for there are no other
hints in Neolithic Shetland of contacts with Malta, or indeed the
Mediterranean.

It is of course far from certain that Yoxie and Stanydale were
temples in the modern sense. All that can be inferred is that they were
not normal dwelling sites, nor were they tombs. They may have been
secular in function, perhaps meeting places for the community, or the
residences of important personages.

Apart from the temple sites, over seventy Neolithic house sites
have been recognised, and in one case, Isleburgh I, a house, heel cairn
and field are all found associated. In the house series it is possible to
recognise early examples which are large with thick walls, and later
types with smaller areas and thin walls. The earlier houses, of which
the Ness of Gruting is a good example, have the main chamber
scooped slightly into the slope of the hillside, have a recess at the end
and sometimes have small benches or beds. The later houses, of which
Wiltrow is typical, have two deep recesses on either side of the
chamber and a compartment at the end, giving them a trefoil plan. In
all, the hearth is placed centrally in the main chamber.

The inhabitants of these houses were essentially crofters, probably

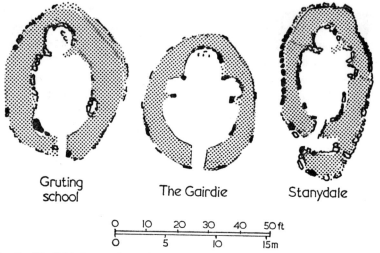

Gruting school   The Gairdie   Stanydale

0   10   20   30   40   50ft
0   5   10   15m

Fig 18   Neolithic house plans, Shetland

little different in their way of life from the Shetlanders of a couple of centuries ago. At the Ness of Gruting a considerable quantity of barley was found preserved by being charred, and animal bones include those of sheep, oxen and ponies. Arrowheads are rare, implying that hunting played a small part, and fishing is only attested by the steatite float plugs already mentioned. Often the houses are isolated, but **they** may be found in groups up to four in number. Associated with them are fields, edged with stone dykes and measuring between 60 and 260ft in their greatest extent. Heaps of land-gathered stones are associated with the fields, just as they are a feature today of the crofting landscape. Of unknown date, but probably in part contemporary with the Neolithic houses, are mounds of burnt stones, which may be associated with outdoor communal cooking places.

The Neolithic sites of Shetland are difficult to date since the associated finds on the whole are peculiar to Shetland, and few datable 'imports' can be recognised. The problem is further complicated by the stone tools that relate to the already mentioned 'circum-

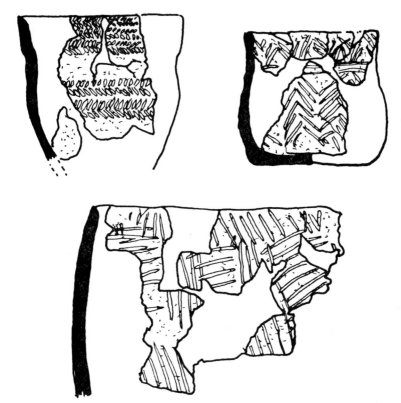

Fig 19   Neolithic pottery, Ness of Gruting, Shetland (after Calder). Scale about ⅖

polar' tradition, through which in the hunter-fisher communities of
the Arctic Circle, Mesolithic or Upper Palaeolithic ways survive due to
extreme conservatism, resulting from difficult living conditions and
relative isolation. There are however a few clues to suggest that the
Neolithic houses and temples were in occupation as early as the first
half of the second millennium BC. There are some fragments of
Beaker pottery from Stanydale, and Beaker pottery influence is
apparent on some of the richly decorated pottery from the house at
Ness of Gruting. Some pottery too closely resembles Neolithic pottery

73

in the Hebrides, while a number of small objects, such as a leaf-shaped arrowhead and a pumice pendant from Stanydale, ground-stone axes and battle axes, all point to an early period of use contemporary with the chambered-tomb users of Orkney and elsewhere (Fig 19).

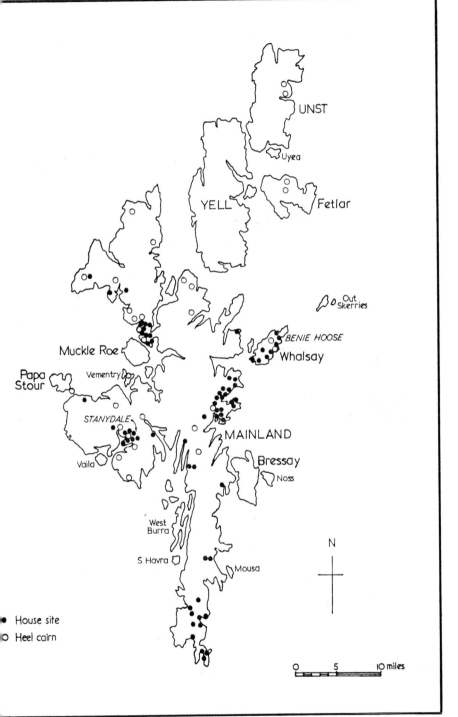

Fig 20 *Neolithic house sites and heel cairns in Shetland*

CHAPTER 3

The Bronze Age and Its Beginnings

The discovery of metalworking opened up new landscapes for early man, for copper, the first metal to be used for edge tools, was relatively scarce and the techniques necessary to fashion it into even simple shapes required skills of an order not possessed by Neolithic artisans. Prospecting is an inevitable preliminary to the finding of copper ore, and gave man a new awareness of his environment. The first prospectors had to learn to detect the taste of copper in the fast-flowing streams from the hills, and to recognise the natural phenomena that indicate the possible presence of cuprous deposits. Neolithic man was fortunate in that many stones could be used instead of flint for shaping arrowheads, but there was no substitute for copper, and the search for it led to widespread travel and trade, and to the emergence of new centres of power and wealth.

EARLY BRONZE AGE

Although rare, almost pure native copper was not unknown in the ancient world and was hammered into small objects in its cold state. The early smiths who worked local copper probably regarded it merely as an unusual stone with malleable qualities—the art of casting was, as will be seen, a later development.

It is perhaps not a coincidence that copper metallurgy appears first in regions where painted pottery was made, since no household hearth would have been hot enough to reduce the metal even to a soft state. In the kilns required for the firing of painted pottery a sufficient heat was present, and it is quite likely that the art of smelting was dis-

76

STONES OF STENNESS

R 72

Fig 21   *The Stenness Stones, Orkney*

covered by the accidental smelting of copper ore in such kilns. The technique was not spread from a central source but seems to have arisen quite independently in several areas, initially before 6000 BC. The site which holds the present record for producing the earliest evidence of copper-smelting is Çatal Hüyük in Turkey. Two thousand years later copper working was to be found in Anatolia, Iran and Palestine, while in Europe a separate tradition in the Balkans and round the Black Sea was producing sophisticated metal tools around 3500 BC. A millennium later still metallurgy appears in the Iberian peninsula. Compared with that of farming, the spread of metalworking was not fast; for instance it did not reach Britain until after 2000 BC, some 1,500 years after the first smiths in Europe practised their art. This seems at first surprising. However it must be remembered that whereas farming skills were common knowledge in a community, those of the smith were probably the prized inheritance of an élite, the secrets being transmitted from a few to a chosen few. The metal worker was an exalted member of early Bronze Age society.

The first non-ferrous metallurgy was confined to copper. Soon however it was discovered that when copper is cast in a closed mould it contains bubbles of free oxygen, which weaken the metal and prevent complex castings being made. The addition of 10 per cent of tin prevents these bubbles being released and also hardens the metal. Thus, rare though tin was, gradually bronze replaced copper as the material chosen for edge tools.

Beaker folk in Europe

The people who were to introduce copper-working to Britain, including the Northern Isles, are a group generally known to archaeologists as the Beaker folk, on account of the distinctive pottery vessel that indicates their presence. This was a bell-shaped pot with thin walls, usually well-fired to a reddish brown. Decoration usually was made by pressing twisted cord horizontally on the clay before firing. The Beaker folk migrations in Europe are one of the very interesting and puzzling folk-movements in prehistory.

The origins of the beakers and their makers are probably to be sought around the Gulf of Lyons. The earliest examples show a combination of features found in two Lyonnais types of pottery—Neolithic impressed ware and Chassey ware. It is difficult to determine how early the first beakers were being made in this area, though a date prior to 2500 BC would probably be reasonably correct. Decoration of impressed cord and also combs was used on the earliest 'bell' beakers, and both types of decoration were taken across Europe with the migrants. The Beaker people expanded from their homeland in four directions: into Iberia and north Africa, across to the Mediterranean islands, and northwards into central Europe by way of the Atlantic seaboard and Rhine on the one hand and the Rhine and Danube on the other.

North of the Rhine and the Low Countries, another group of people flourished before 2000 BC, who were to play an important part in the development of the later Beaker folk. Originating in the south Russian steppes, these Battle Axe people as they are called introduced a variety of new elements into northern Europe: they buried their dead singly in a crouched position in contrast to the collective burials of the megalithic chambered tombs; a new warlike strain appeared in the population for which the most striking archaeological evidence are the stone shaft-hole battle axes in their graves; almost certainly they were responsible for the introduction of the wheel and new varieties of metal objects. Their pottery vessels were similar to the 'bell' beakers, with cord-impressed ornamentation on the upper part. Thus, once the Beaker people were established in northern Europe, they acquired by fusion some of the cultural traits of the Battle Axe folk: the rite of single burial was adopted; the beakers themselves were modified; new types of objects such as tanged copper daggers, stone wrist-bracers for archery and possibly 'V-perforated' buttons resulted.

Originally there were seven Beaker groups in Britain which eventually merged into three. The whole pattern of the settlements is similar to that of the Anglo-Saxon invaders, although Beaker people unlike the Saxons did not confine their activities to Britain. The first migrations did not affect Scotland, though at a fairly early date a group from the middle Rhine settled on the British east coast from the Thames to the Lowlands. The first extensive Scottish settlement occurred at a period when the two cultures of Battle Axe and Beaker people had merged, and is to be found in the Moray Firth area and the Borders; in England it is found in the Yorkshire Wolds. The Veluwe area of the Netherlands was the homeland of the most important settlers in Scotland at this period, the beakers it produced being the ancestors of all subsequent northern beaker forms.

The Beaker people were farmers, with a probable emphasis on pastoralism. Much controversy surrounds Beaker houses in Britain. Few have been excavated and there is little conclusive evidence. At one time it was thought that Neolithic houses were rectilinear while those of the Beaker folk were round. Yet the evidence from recently excavated sites like Belle Tout in Sussex suggests that the Beaker people may have built rectilinear dwellings as well as round and may also have sometimes surrounded them with earth banks.

Metal technology brought to Britain by the Beaker people seems to have been limited to the casting of simple copper objects in open moulds and the wide use of stone tools continued.

Beaker folk in Orkney (Fig 22)

Although it is indisputable that the Beaker folk reached Orkney and Shetland, the scarcity of their pottery suggests that they were few in number. They seem to have mixed more with the native population there than in many of the areas they settled, and there is some evidence that they were even buried in the local chambered tombs. Beaker sherds were found in two of the stalled cairns, Calf of Eday Long and Knowe of Yarso, while both Knowe of Yarso and Unstan have yielded barbed and tanged flint arrowheads of a type usually associated with the Beaker people. Other immigrants were buried in single cists or 'coffins' constructed from stone slabs set on edge, such as those found at Skatness, Shetland.

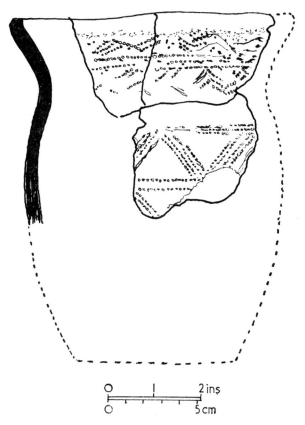

Fig 22   Beaker, Rinyo

Henge monuments in England

The ritual monuments of Britain known as henges have close connections with the Beaker people. Although the name is derived from
the famous and spectacular Stonehenge, it is perhaps misleading since
elaborate stone settings are exceptional. Henges are non-defensive,
with banks and ditches. With few exceptions they fall into two categories: those with single entrances belonging to late Neolithic times,
and those with two entrances which were built by the Beaker folk.

81

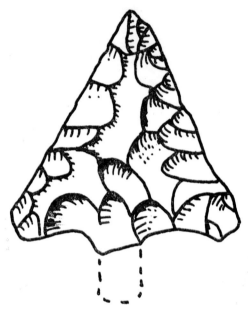

Fig 23 Beaker arrowhead from Unstan, Orkney. Scale: $\frac{4}{1}$

Henges show marked similarities to the late Neolithic 'causewayed camps' like Windmill Hill which, as has been seen, consisted of circular banks and ditches broken by entrances or causeways. These earthworks were not camps in the usual sense, but local rallying points where ceremonies and ritual feasts took place. A variety of similar enclosures existed in Britain, of which henges are one class. In the lowland zone where stone was scarce, timber was sometimes used for associated structures; the classic example is Woodhenge on Salisbury Plain. The function of the timber structures was sometimes funerary, though a few may have been roofed 'temples', and they were all religious in inspiration.

Single-entranced henges, then, were the earliest; the first building of Stonehenge was of this kind. Double-entranced henges were constructed near water and were more oval in plan. Some henges are

extremely large, up to 1,700ft in diameter, and often, like those of
Avebury, Dorchester, Huntingtower and Stonehenge, are part of a
complex pattern of monuments with subsidiary burials, pits and
earthworks. A few of the more sizeable have small 'daughter' circles
within them. This is the case at Avebury and at Durrington Walls,
which along with Woodhenge is part of the Stonehenge complex.

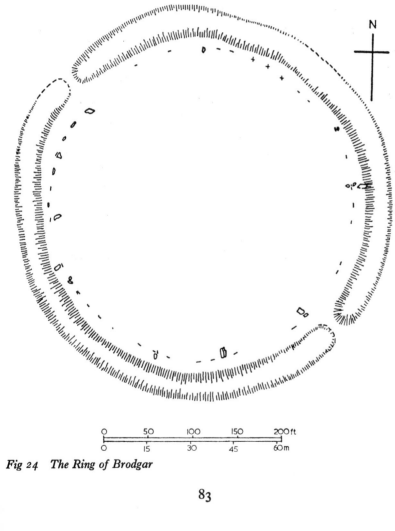

Fig 24 The Ring of Brodgar

Henges in Orkney

Orkney has two henges with associated stone circles, both of which have double entrances, but which have not so far been proven of Beaker origin. They are the Ring of Brodgar and the Stenness Stones, which seem to have belonged to an extensive religious assemblage centring on Loch Stenness. In an area of 2 square miles are to be found four chambered tombs, two henges, other groups of standing stones, single stones and a number of cairns, barrows and mounds.

The Ring of Brodgar encloses an area of 120yd in diameter and has a subsidiary circle of some twenty-seven standing stones, though there were probably about sixty originally. The ditch of the earthwork is about 30ft wide and 6ft deep, while one stone of the circle stands to a height of 15ft and six others to over 10ft (Fig 24; Pl 5a).

Avebury is in many ways similar to Brodgar, except that it has several circles of stones within the earthwork, and there were four not two entrances. It was undoubtedly built by the Beaker folk and has a processional way of double standing stones called the Kennet Avenue, comparable to the single line of stones that links the Ring of Brodgar to the Stenness Stones (Figs 25, 26).

The ditch of the Stenness Circle is now barely visible, and only four stones are standing. The curious trilithon which is so prominent was the result of a 1906 'restoration' of fallen stones. Such an arrangement

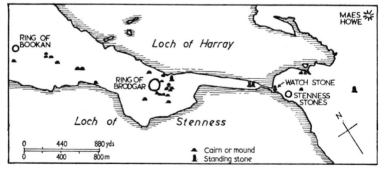

Fig 25 The Stenness region

5a   The Ring of Brodgar henge monument, Orkney
5b   Clickhimin, Shetland, the 'blockhouse'

was inspired by the chambered tombs and would never have existed
in the original circle. The highest of these stones is 17ft, and it will be
noticed that these are large compared to those in the sarsen circle at
Stonehenge which are a mere 13½ft on average.

It may at first seem pointless to draw comparisons between monuments so far apart at Brodgar and Stonehenge. But, strange as it may
seem, there is some evidence to support the theory that when the circle
of trilithons was being constructed at Stonehenge there was contact
between Wessex and Orkney. Stonehenge as we know it (its third
building phase) was the supreme achievement of the Wessex culture
of southern England, which may have had contacts as far afield as
central Europe and Brittany. At present the Wessex culture is the
subject of considerable debate among archaeologists, who are not
agreed as to its duration or precise status, the present controversy over
radiocarbon dating (see the note on chronology at the start of this book)
complicating the issue further. However long it lasted, it is apparent
that its contacts were very widespread, and some kind of contact with
the east Mediterranean, whether or not it was with the Minoan or
Mycenaean world (or possibly both), cannot be doubted in the light
of the most recent research. In view of this, Orkney seems hardly
remote.

The evidence for Wessex influence can be seen in Orkney burials of
a type known as bell-barrows. These are mounds heaped up on the
centre of a level area and encircled with a ditch, leaving a berm. The
type is distinctive of Wessex (though an outlier was recently excavated at
Earl's Barton, Northamptonshire), and a separate development of the
same type in Orkney seems unlikely. The best documented of the
Orkney sites is the largest of the Knowes of Trotty, a group of barrows
on Mainland. When this was opened last century a cremation burial
was found associated with an amber necklace and four gold objects,
usually interpreted as 'sun discs' but which are more probably base
mounts for cone-shaped objects. Although possible parallels might be
sought elsewhere, these can be paralleled from a Wessex grave, while
amber spacer plates for the necklace from the same grave can best be

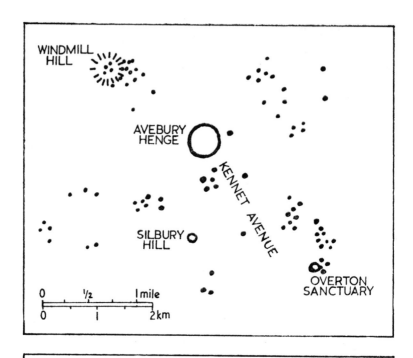

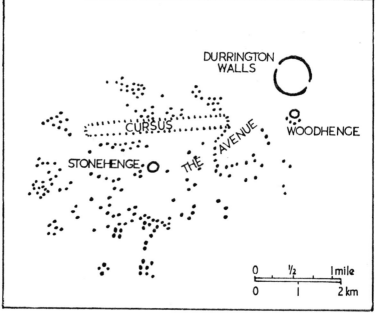

Fig 26 *Stonehenge and Avebury regions (dots indicate barrows)*

paralleled at Upton Lovell in Wiltshire and Oakley Down in Dorset. From elsewhere in Scotland other 'Wessex imports' have been recorded.

How the monuments were built

The stones were probably quarried some distance from the sites, and dragged on rollers or sledges. A block of 3 tons would require twenty men to pull it, and an enormous effort to erect. Most stones were dressed with the simplest equipment—stone chisels and wedges—though metal had been used in the final dressing of Stonehenge. The stones would have been slid up ramps and tipped into pits dug to receive them then hauled into place with levers, and packing stones rammed into place.

A quarry for stones of prehistoric date is known from Vestra Field in the west of the Orkney Mainland. A number of blocks lie embedded in the turf on the hillslope, while one is propped up as though ready for moving. Although probably for standing stones, the quarry may have been used for blocks for chambered-tomb building.

Standing stones

There are no stone circles in Shetland (nor for that matter any simple earthwork henges) though there are a few single standing stones, just as there are quite a number of such standing stones in Orkney. The purpose of the stone circles and single standing stones is enigmatic, and probably incapable of solution. Although henges proper belong to the late Neolithic/Beaker period in Britain, the custom of erecting standing stones, either singly or in circles, without the ditch that characterises a henge continued in the early Bronze Age. Probably there is no single explanation to account for them. Settings of standing stones in various parts of the country are found associated with funerary monuments; they can form circles around burial mounds or graves dug into level ground, though it is not always certain whether their primary function was to enclose these graves.

Recently a careful study has been made of circles of standing stones, from which it has been deduced that they appear to be deliberately oriented and are laid out in accordance with a particular unit of measurement—the so-called 'megalithic yard'. From this it has been further suggested that they are the products of a sophisticated knowledge of mathematics, and were used as primitive 'computers' or observatories. While it must be admitted that such conclusions are based on accurate measurement and observation, unlike the wild speculations of the past, the problems are complex, and it is as yet too early to be certain of the extent of Bronze Age mathematics.

Metalwork in the Northern Isles

It must not be imagined that the arrival of some Beaker settlers and the cultural contact with mainland Scotland that possibly followed resulted in the Northern Isles becoming fully metal using. Metalwork long remained rare there, and most of the population continued the way of life established by their Neolithic ancestors.

Bronze, as opposed to copper, probably first appeared in the Northern Isles around 1800 BC. Early Bronze Age finds are few; an axe and three daggers from Orkney and a solitary tanged dagger from Shetland make up the list (Fig 27). Middle Bronze Age bronzes are as rare—a spearhead and a tanged razor in the remains of its wooden sheath come from an Orcadian barrow at Laughton's Knowe, Holm, while a solitary steatite mould for casting flanged axes shows that, by

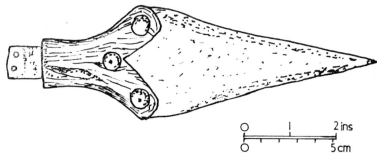

Fig 27   Early Bronze Age dagger, Wasbister, Orkney (after Henshall)

the middle Bronze Age, metalworking was being carried out in Orkney. In Shetland, middle Bronze Age metalwork finds are as few, the only recorded examples being a razor and a blade.

Bronze Age pottery in the Northern Isles

In mainland Scotland different types of pots occurred when beakers were still being made and continued after they had gone out of use. The first type is known quite simply as a food vessel, because it was probably used as a container for offerings of food buried with the dead. Food vessels are thick-walled and squat, with relief and impressed decoration. Broadly contemporary with these are the cinerary urns, that are, as their name suggests, usually found containing cremation burials. They are of a number of different forms and are widespread in highland Britain and Ireland. Like the food vessels, cinerary urns are probably a continuation of late Neolithic traditions.

The Bronze Age pottery in the Northern Isles appears as a separate sequence from that of the mainland; although there are affinities between the cinerary urns of both regions, the Northern Isles have their own variants. A local feature in Orkney is the use of steatite to temper the clay, and in some cases the urns are of carved steatite itself (Fig 28).

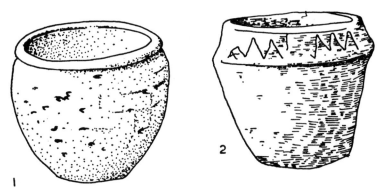

Fig 28 Bronze Age cinerary urns
   1 Clestrain, Stronsay, Orkney, made of steatite
   2 Flemington, Shetland

Bronze Age burials

Frequently the cinerary urns of the Northern Isles are found in stone cists. A number of the Orcadian cists seem to have been used on more than one occasion, as at West Puldrite, where two bodies were pushed to one side to make room for a later burial. An important and unique series of cists have two storeys, and it is not unknown to find cists within cists. Although cists usually contain cremations, inhumations are not unknown.

Very small cists (under 2ft square) are found in the Northern Isles with cremations in correspondingly tiny pottery or steatite vessels. The original late Bronze Age date attributed to these has recently been questioned, archaeologists now preferring one in the early Bronze Age. The result is that no pottery can be ascribed to the middle Bronze Age in the Northern Isles.

Continuity in Shetland

Although the term 'Bronze Age' is used for the period under discussion, it was not until late on that metal implements actually became widely used: life in the Shetlands went on much as it had always done. Stone remained the chief material for equipment. A few Shetland stone axes have splayed blades imitating the hammered edge of metal tools, tangible testimony to the continuation of old and new side by side. Slate was also used in making knives, choppers and clubs—the latter a Shetland speciality.

The basis of the economy was mixed farming. Querns were used for grinding the grain into flour. Cultivated plants, which included barley, provided a supplement to a diet of mutton or lamb. Two kinds of sheep were kept, one akin to the Soay breed and the other similar to the modern Shetland variety. Pony bones suggest that even by this early date the Shelty had been domesticated. Fishing was popular, and seabirds and walrus were hunted.

It is a well-known archaeological fact that in some regions societies tend to be more conservative than in others, continuing the same way of life, making the same types of things, for millennia. Not surprisingly therefore there are close parallels between house types over what appear to be prohibitive spans of time. The tradition in Shetland can be traced from the megalithic tombs mentioned in the last chapter through the Neolithic dwellings to the Bronze Age courtyard houses. Excavations at the Benie Hoose (see p 70) indicate occupation in the Bronze Age extending possibly into the early Iron Age, with only five very slight modifications in plan. This type of continuity can best be illustrated in the late Bronze Age settlement at Jarlshof, which also provides an excellent picture of life in the Bronze Age.

LATE BRONZE AGE

In continental Europe

Before considering Jarlshof and the late Bronze Age in the Northern Isles it is necessary to discuss the late Bronze Age in continental Europe.

Although there was contact between Britain and Europe in the Bronze Age, Bronze Age Britain is characterised by the development of native communities which acquired only from time to time new elements from the continent. Until around 1200 BC a similar situation seems to have existed in mainland Europe, and the archaeology of the early and middle Bronze Age does not indicate any large-scale folk movements. Around 1250 BC however there were a series of major upheavals both in the east Mediterranean and in mainland Europe. Soldiers of fortune from the mainland, who may indeed have been one element in the hotch-potch of raiders known as the 'Peoples of the Sea' who caused havoc in Egypt, probably came back to their homeland with new ideas and technological skills. Certainly around this time the first appearance of, for instance, forts and beaten metalwork is found in Bronze Age Europe, while the development of the sword led to a new age in the history of warfare. About this time too the transition from inhumation to cremation burial in cinerary urns occurred in cemeteries in central Europe. Probably this was not the result of the arrival of cremating immigrants as has sometimes been suggested, but the re-assertion of an old tradition. Whatever their origins, the

93

Urnfield people as they are called spread fairly rapidly from their original centre, taking with them many of the new techniques.

The Urnfield people are the largest group in late Bronze Age Europe, and they penetrated even Italy and the Iberian peninsula. It is almost certain they spoke a form of Celtic. This can be demonstrated by the distribution of certain early forms of Celtic placenames in areas which were not settled by later Celts.

In Scotland

The late Bronze Age in Scotland is characterised by the appearance of leaded bronze—the lead made the bronze harder and also meant that more objects could be made from the same amount of bronze metal. It is also characterised by the widespread occurrence of founders' hoards of scrap metal, which for some reason were never melted down. The phases of the late Bronze Age have been named after various hoards.

An important feature of the Scottish late Bronze Age is the contact that is apparent between the north-east and the continent, and various imported objects can be attributed to this phase. In the final phase, called the Covesea after a characteristic find from the Sculptor's Cave at Covesea in Morayshire, it is possible to recognise a class of coarse, flat-rimmed, bucket-shaped pots, which on account of their shape are known as 'flat-rimmed ware'. This pottery, like the various categories of imported metalwork, seems to originate in the Urnfield cultures of the continent. Its precise ancestry is in doubt, but might well have come from Germany where much of the metalwork seems to originate. The Covesea Phase, which began around 700 BC, also saw the appearance of the first hill forts in Scotland, which have timber-laced ramparts and which seem again to have origins in Urnfield Europe.

Jarlshof and the late Bronze Age

Until the last century all that was visible of the site of Jarlshof was the ruined seventeenth-century house named 'Jarlshof' by Sir Walter Scott in his novel *The Pirate*. In 1896 however a series of heavy storms eroded the huge mound on which the house stood, and revealed

94

hidden walls in the sand. This discovery led to a number of excavations over the years which showed occupation from the Stone Age to the seventeenth century, with breaks only in the early Iron Age and later Middle Ages. The site at present covers 3 acres, and is quite possibly more extensive still. It is easy to understand why Jarlshof

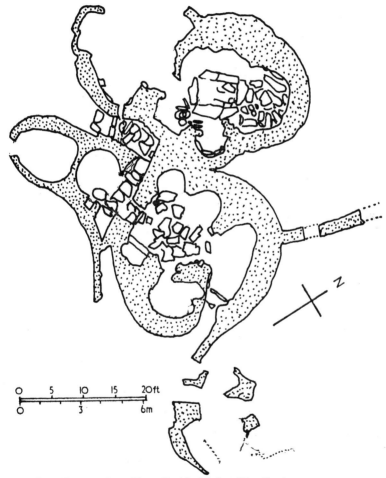

Fig 29   Late Bronze Age village, Jarlshof (after Hamilton)

was chosen by so many successive people. Sumburgh Head on which it lies is the first point of land reached by seafarers sailing north from Orkney. Navigation is helped by the prominent headland and the excellent harbour, while abundant fresh water and grazing land add to the pleasantness of life.

The earliest settlement consisted of an oval stone-built hut surrounded by a wall. The occupants burnt peat on their fires and ate meat and shellfish. The fate of this building was the same as that of subsequent settlements—it was engulfed by windblown sand.

The next development in the Jarlshof story was the village of courtyard houses established around 700 BC. These Bronze Age courtyard houses differ from their Neolithic predecessor only in that they are more regular and specialised, with a more complex internal arrangement (Fig 29; Pl 4b). Cattle were stalled within the dwelling—a whalebone ring set in the wall was probably used for tethering. In one of the Jarlshof houses a hollow in the floor of one of these stalls seems to bear witness to the earliest known instance of the collection of manure for fertiliser in Britain. Internally, stalling was the outcome of climatic change, for about 1000 BC the weather became colder and wetter. This seems to have led to the abandonment of hill-grazing country and the higher fields in favour of the sheltered coastal bays.

Bronze Age economy was more pastoral than that of earlier periods, with flocks of sheep as well as cattle and pigs. Corn was grown and ground in the traditional trough-shaped querns. Steatite bowls were exported to Orkney and points and pins for leather-working were made from bone. Stone axes, adzes, saw-edged blades, pounders and shovels of sandstone or slate remain as the material proof of considerable industry.

The pottery characteristic of the Bronze Age village at Jarlshof belongs to the 'flat-rimmed' type, and related pottery has been found at Clickhimin in Shetland, where there is a hint in the tall shape of some of the pots of influence from the long established Northern Isles series of cinerary urns. The same type of pottery has been found in the late Bronze Age settlement at Skaill, Deerness, Orkney, where a building of the period is at present being excavated, while a settlement at Calf of Eday has produced finds (but no pottery) of a similar type to those at Jarlshof (Fig 30).

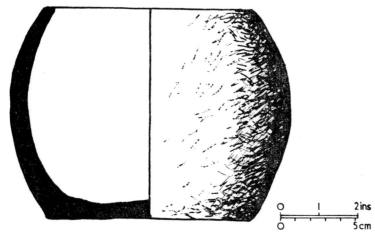

Fig 30   Flat-rimmed ware pot, late Bronze Age, Jarlshof (after Hamilton)

The Jarlshof bronze smith (Fig 31)

Fortunately for archaeology a bronze smith moved to Jarlshof around 650 BC and his workshop has been investigated. His products are in keeping with Adabrock metalwork elsewhere. The repertoire of the Jarlshof smith however suggests also Irish connections, and it is conceivable that he emigrated to Shetland to ply his trade at a time when iron was already becoming familiar elsewhere in Britain.

Some 200 pieces of clay moulds were recovered, during excavation, that had originally been used for casting socketed axes, swords, a gouge and a so-called 'sunflower pin' (a pin with a broad flat head and bent neck). The moulds had been set in a casting pit filled with clean sand, and there was a supply of clay and a stone trough. Casting, as was often the case during the Bronze Age, was done by making a pattern, probably of wood, and forming the two halves of the mould round it. The halves would then have been wrapped in a coarser clay and filled with molten metal. The alternative method was to make a wax model which was encased in clay and the wax melted out—the *cire perdue* method.

Raw material for this workshop could have been acquired locally in the form of copper ore, but tin would have had to be imported unless the metal from old tools was melted down and re-used.

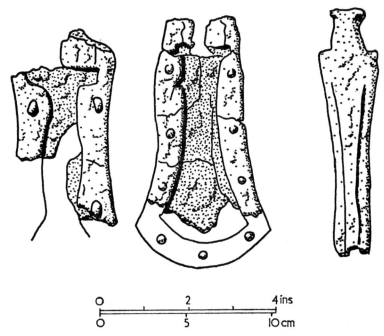

Fig 31   Late Bronze Age moulds, Jarlshof (after Hamilton)

CHAPTER 4

The Iron Age: Stone Forts, Brochs and Earth-Houses

The last chapter dealt with a period which in conventional terms would have been called Bronze Age. The rarity of metal however in the Northern Isles at least until after 1000 BC suggests that in these communities the use of metal played little part in the economy. The evidence from both Orkney and Shetland shows how Neolithic cultures continued to exist long after non-ferrous metallurgy was well established elsewhere in Britain and Europe. Most of the metalwork from the Northern Isles could have been imported, or the work of itinerant smiths—in either case the indigenous peoples made little use of it in their daily lives.

Just as there is no sharp transition from a Neolithic to a Bronze Age economy, there is no sharp transition to an Iron Age either. Iron-working is considerably more complex than the fashioning of copper or bronze. Whereas bronze can be cast, iron until the advent of modern techniques had to be wrought or forged. Its present-day hardness is achieved by tempering and quenching, or by the addition of carbon to produce steel. Strange though it may seem, tempering and quenching did not make their appearance in ironworking until the Middle Ages, and though the Romans occasionally made objects of steel by accident, ferrous metallurgy remained at much the same stage in Europe from its first appearance to medieval times.

Iron technology was not developed at an early stage since ferrous edge tools could not better bronze, although they were harder than unalloyed copper. Just as native copper was worked before the advent of copper metallurgy, so was native iron, which can be found in meteoric fragments. Sometimes smelted iron was used in the Near East in the third millennium BC—an iron dagger was among the finds from a rich burial at Alaça Hüyük in Turkey. When bronze replaced copper for edge tools, iron seems to have been used only for ornaments. It was regarded as a precious metal, and even as late as the time of Tutankhamun (1357–1349 BC) was included among the golden riches in his tomb. The Hittites were probably the first to see the chief advantage of iron over copper, namely its relative abundance. The centre of their empire in Turkey was particularly rich in iron ore, and

Fig 32   Broch of Mousa, Shetland

they were working it on a moderate scale by c 1500 BC, and by 1300 BC it was an important commodity in their trade.

With the break-up of the Hittite empire the secret of ironworking was dispersed in the Aegean, where it was established by the eleventh century BC. Independently, somewhere to the north of the Black Sea, another centre of ferrous metallurgy developed around the ninth or eighth century BC and from here the expansion of steppe nomads introduced iron objects into northern and central Europe.

The later Urnfield people learned of ironworking, and the impact of the Eurasiatic nomads on the Urnfield peoples was one factor which led to the development of Celtic Hallstatt culture of the early Iron Age. The early Hallstatt culture, which centred on Czechoslovakia, was Bronze Age, iron being a considerable rarity, but by 700 BC the culture was fully iron using.

The earliest Iron Age in Shetland

The Bronze Age settlement at Jarlshof was succeeded by a second village of round houses, called by the excavators Bronze Age Village II but which may now more aptly be regarded as Iron Age Village I, an iron based economy being increasingly adopted. This village, which was built over the remains of the first, had souterrains or underground storage passages attached to the houses, and from it comes a new type of pottery with sharp shoulders and concave necks, the rims being hammer-headed and often punctured with impressions. Some of this pottery was thin, and had a black polished surface. It is related to the earliest Iron Age pottery found in England and Wales, though some rather similar ware was used in Heathery Burn cave in County Durham, a late Bronze Age settlement of the seventh century BC. Elsewhere in Scotland the pottery is virtually unknown, and it may denote the presence of later groups of continental people. The profile of the shouldered vessels probably originally imitated metal proto-types.

The houses in this village were circular, with partition walls. Iron slag attests the presence of ironworkers, though some bronze working was still carried out and a few products of the late Bronze Age smith's work seem to have been still in use. Chronologically, there seems to have been little gap between the late Bronze Age and the Iron Age villages. Other finds from the Iron Age village included steatite armlets and stone beads and whorls, and it is possible that the armlets are steatite versions of jet types which turn up on some early Iron Age sites in England, notably the Yorkshire sites of Staple Howe and Scarborough.

Further north on Mainland, a comparable settlement is known at Clickhimin. The new settlers found the old Bronze Age dwelling in a sufficiently good state of repair to use it as an outhouse, erecting a new round house of Jarlshof type with a wall 5 to 7ft thick and an internal diameter of about 25ft. The radial piers were possibly intended to support a gallery running round a central space where a hearth would have blazed—certainly the thickness of the walls suggests the building was of some height (Fig 33).

The fact that neither Jarlshof nor Clickhimin were defensive at this period suggests that the settlement was fairly peaceful and the immigrants mixed with the older Bronze Age stock. They continued to farm and fish, and to burn peat on their fires. At Jarlshof the old style of trough-quern persisted. Steatite was probably quarried on a larger scale, and at Clickhimin, a steatite lamp belonging to this period was found.

THE FORT BUILDERS

Possibly as early as the seventh century BC there was another immigration to Scotland from western France of people of Urnfield origin, bringing with them pottery with fluted and everted rims, which is found as far afield as Dun Mhor Vaul in Tiree and Clickhimin (Fig 33). These people were responsible for replacing the early Iron Age farmstead at Clickhimin with a more ambitious project. This was a stone-walled fort, the drystone wall of which ran round the island enclosing an area 138ft by 125ft. The wall is about 10ft thick at its base, and in places stands to about 8ft or more. The wall was broached by an entrance passage 9ft wide and nearly 18ft long, and was thickened at a later stage when the passage was blocked by a wooden door.

7a Midhowe Broch, Rousay, Orkney: the defensive ditch with post-broch hut behind

7b Midhowe Broch, Rousay, Orkney: the intra-mural staircase of the broch

8a Midhowe Broch, Rousay, Orkney: general view from Midhowe Cairn

8b Interior of the broch, Broch of Gurness, Aikerness, Orkney

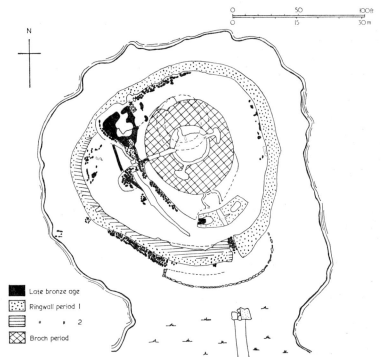

Fig 33 Plan of Clickhimin

It probably had a wall-walk like other stone forts; although this is now missing, a stone staircase built in the wall presumably once gave access to one.

Round the inside of this stone wall, ranges of timber buildings were constructed of lean-to type, the roofs of which would have been supported by a scarcement now missing. There could have been fairly substantial structures projecting above the level of the wall-walk, as the excavator J. R. C. Hamilton has suggested, but this seems un-likely. The roofs of the penthouses were of timber, probably with wooden shingles. Peat mould and manure from the floor of the timber structures suggest that most were byres. The northern end of the first range was probably domestic, since manure and peat mould were absent and instead were found saddle querns and nearby a hearth which, on the evidence of clinker, was used for ironworking. Within the stone fort the earlier Iron Age house probably remained standing, for at a later date it was incorporated into the structure of a broch.

Stone forts of the same general type were probably introduced to the Hebrides around the same time, or slightly later. In response to the rocky environment, the early stone forts there evolved into a new type, built with hollow walls. In this type of construction a double wall is built up with transverse bonding stones. The technique first appears in a series of small Hebridean forts known as 'semi-brochs', and probably evolved in the later fifth or fourth century BC following the arrival in the Hebrides of a group of immigrants from Yorkshire.

The technique of building with hollow walls seems to have spread fairly early to Shetland, and is apparent in the second fort building phase at Clickhimin. All that now exists of the original (incomplete?) fort of this phase is the massive 'blockhouse' (Pl 5b). This is a masonry structure some 43ft by 13½ft, the masonry being built up with a batter on each face, and originally standing to a height of at least 18–20ft. Through the centre ran a passage, rebated for a door nearly 4ft wide by 4ft 3in high, set some 5ft behind the face of the wall and originally secured with a sliding bar. On either side were compartments, which seem to have been entered from above and could therefore not have served as guardchambers. Behind this structure probably stood a timber penthouse. The wall of a small fort probably ran out from the blockhouse, of which only a small part survives due to later disturbance from the building of the broch tower.

Flooding of the islet on which Clickhimin was built resulted in further building operations, including the emergency landing stage, the building up of the interior of the old fort entrance and repair work on its walls. A breakwater was constructed in the south-west quadrant.

Two other forts related to the blockhouse fort at Clickhimin are known in Shetland. At Loch of Huxter a blockhouse entrance still has its associated fort wall, built not with hollow walling but with a single stone rampart as in the first fort at Clickhimin. Like Clickhimin, it stands on an islet approached by a causeway. At Ness of Burgi, not far from Jarlshof, a ruined blockhouse can be seen, defended in front by a rampart and ditch. The position of this fort on a promontory did not necessitate the building of a complete *enceinte* wall. Both Huxter and Burgi have intra-mural chambers, but these, unlike the Clickhimin ones, could be entered at ground level.

The finds from the pre-broch phase at Clickhimin are important, especially since there is no other excavated site of the period in the Northern Isles. Like their predecessors the occupants were farmers, with a variety of possessions. They made stone pounders, pot lids,

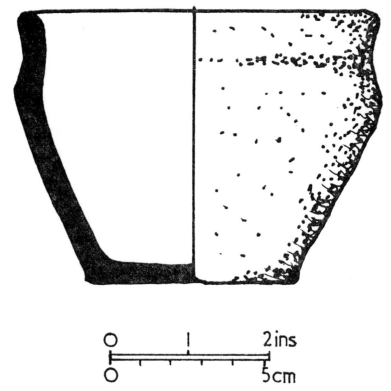

Fig 34 Jarlshof—earliest Iron Age pot

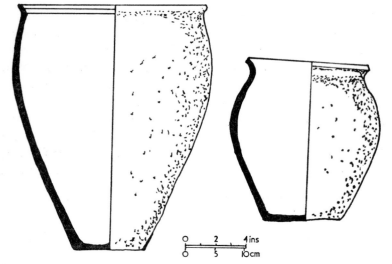

*Fig 35   Fluted rim pot and another pot of stone fort period, Clickhimin
(after Hamilton)*

querns, beads and plaques. They fashioned pins, points, awls, toggles
and pegs all of bone. Weaving continued, and their diet seems to have
had the addition of whales. Finger and toe rings of metal and glass
beads were imports from the south, presumably by way of the west
coast. Slings were used for defence, stone lamps for light.

The pottery shows two elements. First, the fluted-rim ware derived
apparently from a type current in France (see p 102), and second the
old shouldered jars of the type introduced by the earliest Iron Age
farmers. Both traditions seem to have mingled and continue into the
broch period on the site.

THE DEVELOPMENT OF THE BROCHS (Fig 36; Pls 6–8)
Further developments in stone fort architecture were to take place at
the beginning of the first century BC in the Hebrides, following the
arrival there of newcomers from southern England. These developments involved building small hollow-wall forts to a much greater

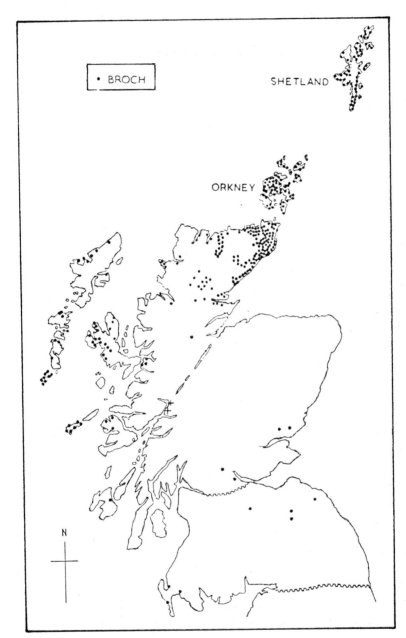

Fig 36 *The distribution of brochs*

height, producing effectively a tower. These forts, known to archaeologists as brochs (the word is derived from a Norse term meaning a fortified place), probably developed in Skye and spread from there very rapidly through the Hebrides and thence to Orkney, where the ready availability of good building stone resulted in brochs being built higher. From Orkney, brochs spread to the northern Scottish mainland (particularly Sutherland and Caithness) and to Shetland. The spread of brochs does not seem to be associated with a corresponding spread of people, for the material culture of the broch dwellers varies according to the region in which they are found, and it is probable that they were built by the local Iron Age people initially under the guidance of itinerant 'architects'.

At their most typical, brochs enclose a central court about 25–35ft in diameter. The enclosing wall was about 12ft thick, and was pierced by a passage with door checks and a bar hole for a thick wooden door. Two intra-mural chambers opened from the entrance passage, one serving as a guardchamber, the other giving access to an internal staircase. From the first-floor level an inner and an outer casement wall rose, bonded with transverse slabs and with an internal staircase to the top of the wall. The inner wall face had a ledge which supported a timber range about 6ft above the floor. Doors from the first or second floor of this range sometimes led through an inner casement to galleries connected with the staircase. Brochs usually had a central well, and at a very late stage in their history had in addition fixed stone furnishings such as water tanks in the floor, slab partition walls, stone cists and fireplaces.

Way of life of the broch people (Fig 38)

The economy of the broch people was primarily agricultural, though it was to some extent supplemented by fishing and whaling. They kept cattle, sheep and pigs, and occasionally hunted deer, seal or sea otter. Their material equipment in the Northern Isles originally consisted of the traditional circumpolar tool-kit of stone and bone—pounders, rubbers, discs and awls. To this was added distinctive pottery of early

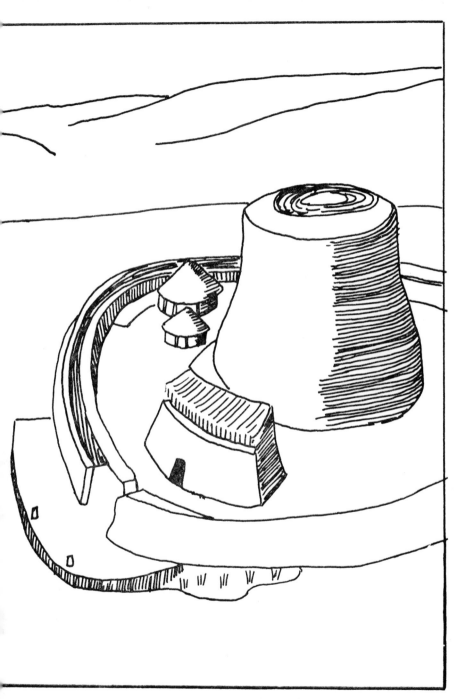

Fig 37 *Reconstruction of Clickhimin in the broch period*

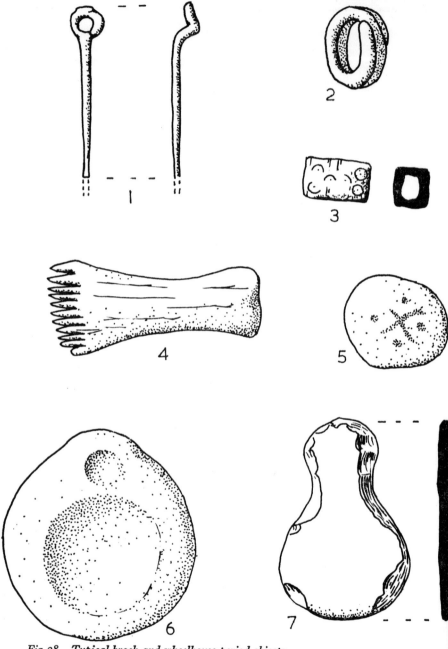

Fig 38 *Typical broch and wheelhouse period objects*
  1 Ring headed pin, Jarlshof   *2 Spiral finger ring, Clickhimin*
  3 Bone dice, Sanday   *4 Weaving comb*
  5 Painted pebble, Clickhimin *6 Stone lamp, Clickhimin*
  7 Stone palette, Clickhimin

Iron Age type which owes its origins both to native traditions in the northern late Bronze/early Iron Age ceramic range and to intrusive elements derived from English Iron Age 'B' cultures. A third element seems to be specialised equipment for making textiles— spindle whorls, bobbins, weaving combs and slotted bones. These appear to be a later addition to the range of equipment of the broch people. Like other Iron Age economies the broch builders worked metal, melting it in triangular clay crucibles.

The brochs were the Iron Age equivalents of the castles of the Middle Ages and, like them, were probably the homes of clan chiefs. It was a troubled age, and not only threats of attack from the south, but civil war between rival chiefs, piracy and even slave raiding may have played a part in the conditions which resulted in their being built. Evidence of the violence of the times was seen at the Broch of Gurness in Orkney, where the bones of two hands were found in a midden, deliberately severed at the wrist. Three rings remained on a finger of one hand, and two on a finger of the other. An Irish folk tale reflects the situation when it describes a legendary hero, Labraid Loinseach, who 'smote eight towers in Tiree, eight strongholds of the men of Skye . . . he ventured upon many of the islands of Orkney'. The capture of hostages and resultant slave raiding are also seen in the Irish stories, notably in the tale of Niall of the Nine Hostages. Although such tales refer to Ireland, it is fairly certain that a similar state of affairs existed in northern Scotland.

Orkney brochs (Figs 39–40)

It would seem that Orkney was particularly powerful in the first two centuries AD, and there is a tradition that in AD 43 Orcadian chiefs concluded a treaty with the Romans. There are 102 brochs in Orkney, of which two, Broch of Gurness at Aikerness on Mainland and Midhowe on Rousay are in the guardianship of the Department of the Environment and displayed to the public.

Midhowe is romantically sited on Rousay, on the edge of the shore between two narrow creeks. On the landward side the broch was

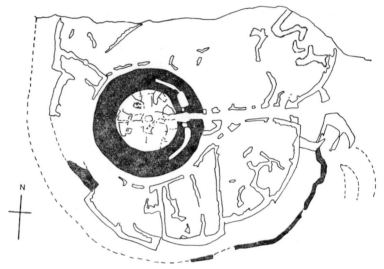

Fig 39   Broch of Gurness, Aikerness

defended by an inner and an outer ditch and adjoining the broch on
the north-west side is a complex of later huts. The broch still rises to a
height of 14ft in places and 13–19ft thick, built up with layers or 'skins'
of masonry. At a later date buttresses were added to the broch wall.
Rock-cut steps provided access to the rocks where boats could have
been launched. Outside the broch, now protected under a glass frame,
is a small stone-built smelting hearth, with masses of iron slag. Other
evidence for metalworking are moulds for casting bronzes and
crucibles, though few metal objects were found in the excavations of
1930–3.

In the second century AD the occupants of the broch must have
taken part in a pillaging expedition to the south, like many of their
contemporaries. Evidence for this takes the form of Roman pottery
and the handle of a Roman bronze saucepan. For a time the broch
seems to have been kept in good repair, and additions were made to the
outer wall. In the transition from war to peace which followed, huts
were built partly out of stone pillaged from the broch.

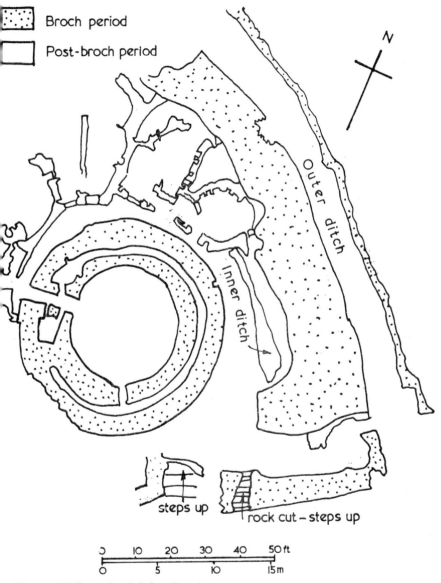

Broch period

Post-broch period

N

Outer ditch

Inner ditch

steps up

rock cut – steps up

	10	20	30	40	50 ft
0		5		10	15 m

Fig 40   Midhowe Broch (after Grant)

A similar sequence of events took place at the Broch of Gurness, which was defended by a series of banks and ditches broken by an entrance causeway facing the entrance passage of the broch. As at Midhowe there was some attempt to renew the fortifications at a fairly late date in the broch's history, when a bastion was built round the broch platform, probably in the second century AD. This phase did not last long, and soon the broch and its defences fell into decay, being engulfed in debris. The ditches were filled in, and on this new ground level a warren of secondary huts was constructed which were occupied until the Viking period.

Shetland brochs

Of the Shetland brochs, the most imposing is that at Mousa, off the Mainland, where the tower still attains a height of over 40ft. As such it is the highest surviving broch in Scotland, and even in its day must have been of exceptional size.

At Clickhimin, the stone fort was replaced by a broch, the building of which appears to have been a matter of some considerable urgency. The work of consolidating the ringwork following the flood was abandoned. Huts were erected for the builders during the initial phase of construction, and one of these contained large bone and antler handles probably belonging to heavy iron-bladed tools on the floor. The broch tower was built in part over the unfinished ringwork, and the 'blockhouse' was refurbished with the addition of a floor between the first and second storeys, reached by a stone staircase inserted into the west gable. The pottery from the broch construction and early occupation levels shows that the native occupants of the fort were not driven out by incoming broch builders, but were themselves a major element in the broch building population. Three types of pottery came from the broch—fluted and plain everted-rim pots with double rims in the fort tradition, heavier pots with finger-pressed bands round the rim which are related to broch pottery in Orkney, and coarse steatitic pots in the native tradition. The neck-band pottery indicates the presence of newcomers from Orkney.

Once built the broch at Clickhimin was occupied for a considerable time. The basic economy was similar to that of the fort builders. Iron was smelted, and some copper was also worked, the metal probably coming from Sandwick, 10 miles away. Steatite and sandstone lamps were fairly common, and the range of bone equipment seems to have been more extensive than before. The population of the broch period was probably similar to that of the fort, and fifty to sixty people could easily have been accommodated on the islet.

Apart from Clickhimin, there are fifteen other sites where brochs replaced stone forts in Shetland.

At Jarlshof, the settlement of earlier Iron Age houses and souterrains was buried under wind-blown sand. The broch builders probably arrived on the site after a period of abandonment, and the broch itself does not appear to have been occupied for very long. It was built with an attached courtyard—unfortunately half of both broch and courtyard have been eroded by the sea, though one intra-mural chamber of what was probably the entrance still survives. The pottery from the broch shows, as at Clickhimin, a mixture of native occupants with incoming people from Orkney who used neck-band ware (Fig 41).

Warfare and the broch builders

The broch builders do not seem to have had very elaborate military equipment—metal weapons being iron and given to rust are absent from brochs. Pebbles, painted with strange dot and line motifs are very probably slingstones, and it has been suggested that the designs are equivalents of the mottoes that sometimes were inscribed on Greek and Roman lead slingshot, like 'take that' or 'strike hard'. Such painted pebbles have been found at Clickhimin and Jarlshof in Shetland, Burrian in Orkney, and on sites on the Scottish mainland.

The main weapon of the broch people seems, however, to have been a type of socketed bone tip which could be attached to a wooden haft with bundles of inflammable material, to form fire-spears. They are not exclusive to the broch people, and are found among other Iron Age societies in England. One set was found with a warrior burial at

Grimsthorpe in Yorkshire, where one point still had its wooden peg in place.

It has been suggested that the broch people were not merely involved in local warfare but also carried on hostilities with the Iron Age inhabitants of the north mainland who occupied timber-laced hillforts—the Abernethy culture. Certainly there is evidence that forts were fired

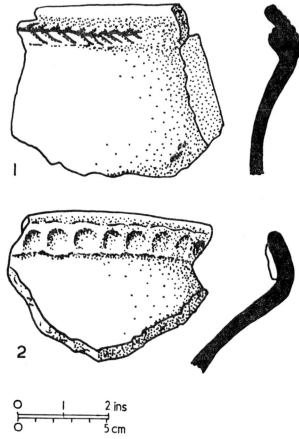

Fig 41   Broch pottery, Shetland (after Hamilton)
1 Cumlins, Olnesfirth   2 Jarlshof

by accident or design in a broad belt from the Dornoch Firth down the Great Glen and the west coast from Loch Broom to the Solway. In this area at least forty forts show signs of vitrification, ie of the partial fusion of the stone wall brought about by intense heat due to the timbers burning and providing draught channels. If the forts were all burned down by accident it would be difficult to explain the distribution pattern, for except for a few outliers the timber-laced forts outside this area do not seem to have been so destroyed. A state of war between the broch people and the Abernethy people would be a very probable explanation were it not for the fact that some broch dwellers of the north mainland seem to have belonged to a regional manifestation of the Abernethy culture. But archaeological cultures do not always indicate political groups, and it is easy to envisage fighting between the mainlanders and the occupants of the Northern Isles over the sea routes to the south, for the broch builders probably required to trade with the south for metal, timber, grain and other commodities, in return for which they no doubt offered sealskins and the other products of the northern waters.

The end of the brochs

It seems likely on present evidence that the brochs continued in use as fortified places only until around the second century AD, though the sites in many cases have produced evidence of occupation continuing until the period of Norse settlement. The cause should probably be seen as a period of peace replacing the previous period of continuing warfare. This happier state of affairs was probably brought about through the fact that the main enemies of the broch builders, the mainlanders, were preoccupied with coping with the forces of military Rome and also, no doubt, acquiring either through trade or theft some of the trappings of Roman materialism. For a time, as already mentioned (p 114), the structures of the old brochs seem to have been kept in good repair, while inside the brochs the open court was divided up into more manageable units with the aid of sandstone partitions; this can be seen both in the Isles, as at Midhowe or Gurness, and at Carn

Liath in Caithness. Gradually however the brochs fell into decay and the stone was used to construct complexes of huts which clustered round the base of the ruined broch and gradually began to encroach upon it, as at Midhowe, Gurness and Lingro in Orkney.

In Shetland, evidence points to a more dramatic transition. At Jarlshof part of the courtyard wall of the broch was taken down to build a roundhouse with some broch-like features, notably an internal timber range. Radial stone piers were inserted at a secondary stage, turning the house into something more akin to the roundhouses of the earlier Bronze and Iron Ages of the Northern Isles. This in turn was replaced with the wheelhouses described in Chapter 5.

EARTH-HOUSES (Figs 42–3)

Brochs were not the only habitation sites of the first centuries AD in the Northern Isles. Another distinctive class of monument found in Orkney, but not in Shetland except for those of the earliest Iron Age phase at Jarlshof, is the earth-house or souterrain. There is a distinctive Orcadian group of these, which are more elaborate and conform to a different plan to those of Jarlshof; they are probably all of a later

Fig 42   Interior of Orcadian earth-house

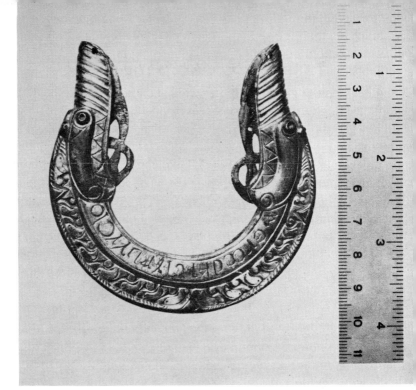

9a   St Ninian's Isle Treasure,
Shetland: strap end with Pictish
inscription

9b   St Ninian's Isle Treasure,
Shetland: sword pommel

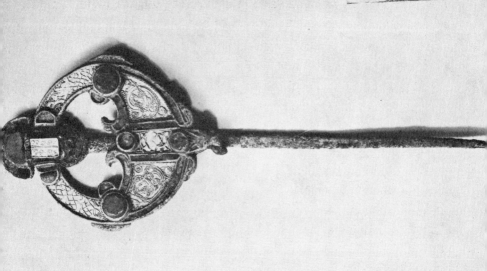

10a The Papil Stone, Shetland

10b The Westness brooch, Rousay, Orkney

date. Of something like twenty-eight sites on Orkney, about fifteen are documented.

Earth-houses are found widespread in many parts of Scotland, Ireland, Cornwall (where they are called fogous), France and even Denmark. As the name suggests they are underground structures, sometimes consisting of a long passage without a proper terminal chamber, sometimes of a short passage terminating in a chamber of impressive character with a slab roof supported by orthostats. A small number of them are merely cavities, oval in shape, a few feet underground. What seems fairly certain is that they are not all of the same date, nor did they all serve the same purpose, and many regional groups can be recognised. Earth-houses are frequently found in or near farmyards, no doubt because the builders were farmers and sited their structures on good agricultural land.

The most characteristic feature of the Orcadian souterrains is the chamber, and in at least one case (Yinstay) there appears to have been no approach passage at all, the entrance to the chamber being made by way of a hatch in the roof of the chamber itself. Where access to the chamber is provided, it is generally a short passage, on average not more than 12ft long, 3ft wide and 2ft 9in high. Only three souterrains have longer passages, the longest being Saverock with a passage 42ft long. In a few cases entrance to the passage was gained by descending a few steps from the ground surface. Some, like Braebister Upper, have external door-checks at the junction of the passage and chamber. The chambers are irregular in shape, but a characteristic feature of most of them is the use of piers or supports for the roof lintels. A few have second chambers, and one even has a third. While most of the chambers were stone walled, a few are simply unlined trenches dug into the clay and sandstone.

At Grain, just outside Kirkwall, a fine example has a bean-shaped chamber with carefully built walls, of which the roof is some 6½ft below ground level. It is approached by a sloping curved passage ending in a series of steps. At Rennibister, which like Grain is open to the public, the roughly hexagonal chamber is reached at the end of an

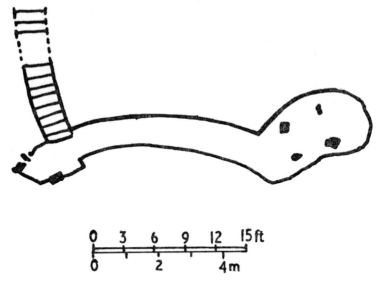

Fig 43 Plan of earth-house at Grain (after R.C.H.A.M.S.)

11½ft passage which terminates with a 2½ft drop to the chamber floor. The chamber has small 'cupboards' in the angles of the side walls, the function of which is unknown. When it was opened the passage was found filled with black earth mixed with shells. The main chamber was free from this blocking, but on the floor were human bones and skulls, four of the latter being placed carefully side by side at the base of one of the four pillars that supported the roof. There were in all the remains of at least six adults and a dozen young people. Presumably the use of the earth-house as a mortuary was secondary and later than the main period of use.

Most of the discoveries from the Orcadian earth-houses are un-informative. The most interesting finds are unfortunately now lost—pottery was found at Gripps and Hatston, while at Grainbank a fish-tailed bone comb was reputedly found. From the descriptions of these finds it seems as though the souterrains were being built and used at least as early as the later broch period. It is possible that they were in use even after the broch period had ended—at St Tredwell's chapel on Papa Westray an earth-house seems to have been built after a broch there had fallen into decay.

Various explanations have been put forward for the earth-houses found in Scotland; some have suggested they were places of refuge, others that they were underground storage rooms for dairy produce, others still that they were underground byres for cattle. In the case of the Orcadian examples the second explanation is the most likely, as they are too small and have too narrow entrances for cattle to be driven into them (and, for that matter, the steps would have been impossible for cattle to negotiate), nor are they ideal as places of retreat.

CHAPTER 5

From Prehistory to History

Around the second or early third century AD the period of broch building came to an end in the Northern Isles. Roman imports provide the date for the beginning of the next phase, which in Shetland is called the 'wheelhouse' period because of the characteristic dwellings. A fragment of glass of the late first or early second century came from the early wheelhouse occupation at Clickhimin, while at Dun Mhor Vaul in Tiree, Roman glass and samian pottery indicate a date in the second century for the end of the broch. The post-broch settlement at Lingro in Orkney produced two coins of Antoninus Pius (AD 138–61), while Roman pottery has been found in secondary occupation levels at Midhowe and Aikerness in Orkney and Keiss in Caithness, all suggesting that the post-broch period of the Scottish Iron Age must begin towards the end of the second century.

WHEELHOUSES (Fig 45)

The wheelhouse culture is a phenomenon of Shetland and the Hebrides; wheelhouses as such do not exist in Orkney, where one finds instead small stone huts more akin to those of the earlier Iron Age. A wheelhouse was a circular building built without mortar and with radial piers reminiscent of the spokes of a wheel, which divided the interior up into compartments. These were roofed about 9 or 10ft above floor level with corbelled slabs. Wheelhouses were on average about 30 to 40ft in diameter, with an open hearth in the centre.

It has been suggested that the Shetland wheelhouses were derived

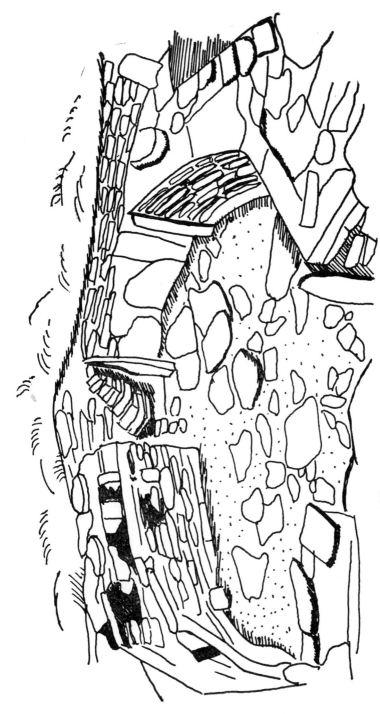

Fig 44 Interior of post-broch hut, Midhowe

from the older stone hut or 'courtyard house' tradition of Bronze Age and Iron Age Shetland, and that the compartments with their radial piers are simply an elaboration of the earlier side cubicles. An alternative suggestion is that the radial piers developed from stone imitations of the supports of the internal timber ranges that may have existed in early examples. The development from this, the aisled wheelhouse, to the wheelhouse proper, probably came about because the aisled construction proved inadequate to support the roof, and in Jarlshof one pier of the aisled wheelhouse was blocked up probably for just this

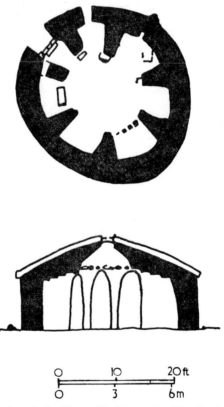

Fig 45   Reconstruction of wheelhouse, Jarlshof (after Hamilton)

reason. Certainly the evidence from this site suggests that the development of the wheelhouse took place in Shetland, for at Jarlshof the true wheelhouse seems to have evolved through a transitional phase in which aisled wheelhouses were constructed, with a gap between the radial piers and the outer wall, tied by stone lintels. The Jarlshof wheelhouse builders were themselves the descendants of the broch builders, and the wheelhouse was to remain the basic house type until the arrival of the Vikings in the late eighth century. At Clickhimin, following the decay of the broch, a wheelhouse was built within the ruin, and wheelhouse occupation of a similar nature is recorded from a number of other broch sites, including Mousa itself and Clumland. From Shetland, the wheelhouse type of dwelling probably spread to the Hebrides, where a local type developed.

It seems likely that the appearance of wheelhouses was associated with social changes. Instead of a large social unit, such as must have been involved in the building of stone forts and brochs, there was a reversion to the smaller family unit throughout the former broch province. Ancestral ties however may have been responsible for the continuity of use of broch sites in many instances in the Northern Isles, even though the crumbling masonry of the broch towers posed a serious threat to the occupants, who must often have lived in terror of a mass of masonry falling from above and crashing through the roof of their home. Not all wheelhouses were built on broch sites, however, and in the Hebrides it would seem that brochs were never used in this way.

The wheelhouse people seem to have been very conservative. Pottery with fluted and double rims continued to be used at Clickhimin, while at Jarlshof the pottery was derived from that of the brochs, though representing a new tradition. There were a few improvements, mainly in farming techniques, and at Jarlshof the field system was modified as a result. Rotary querns replaced the older saddle types and a new tool, a notched slate stick, was introduced to separate the ear from the corn stalk in harvesting. Metalworking was similar to that of the broch period. An iron ring-headed pin together with fragments of moulds and mould gates and iron lumps were found at Jarlshof. The curious painted pebbles which have already been mentioned as the possible slingstones of the broch period, continued to be used.

At Jarlshof and Clickhimin the final, pre-Norse phase of the settlements was very impoverished. At Jarlshof a couple of huts with an associated earth-house were occupied. This earth-house, known as the Passage House, consisted of a sloping passage over 25ft long leading to three chambers, with walls built of upright slabs supporting horizontal facing stones. Initially it was used for habitation, but later appears to have been used as a byre. At Clickhimin, in this phase, there was a tendency to dig huts or storage pits into the earlier middens. During the earlier period the strait which separated the island from Mainland had silted up, and a causeway was built, possibly to provide a means of taking cattle out to the islet. At this time a footprinted stone was brought from somewhere else and re-erected at the threshold of the fort. Such stones with carved footprints are known from elsewhere in Scotland—there is a famous example in the capital of the Dalriadic Scots at Dunadd in Argyll, and another was found on the beach at St Mary's on South Ronaldsay in Orkney. They are traditionally associated with the inauguration of kings, and later in Scottish history it is said that the Lords of the Isles stood on such footprints to be proclaimed. The tradition is also known in Ireland, and may well be a Celtic custom introduced in the early Iron Age. The Clickhimin stone has a circular depression at either end, between the toes and between the heels.

That the wheelhouse period continued in Shetland until the arrival of the Norse is proved by the fact that Norse objects seem mixed with late wheelhouse finds in middens, while associated with wheelhouse period finds at Jarlshof are a rough slab with a cross incised on it and a Pictish symbol stone. From this it can be inferred that at some point in time the wheelhouse people, at Jarlshof at least, became Christian.

The pottery sequence at Jarlshof also implies long continuity. The earliest pottery has flat, roll-top or bead rims and is fine and hard, generally with a reddish colour. At a later stage new shapes appear, made in a buff coloured ware, the most common form being a large open bowl with slightly inverted flat-topped rim. About the same time as the buff ware, a fine grey or grey-black pottery with burnished surface becomes common, fairly globular vessels with sharply everted rims being the most usual. In the latest period, the pottery associated with the Passage House is thin walled and crude, and represents a degenerate form of buff ware. The faces of the pots are pared, and the most common form is a straight-sided jar with a flat or square-sectioned rim (Fig 46).

In Orkney the sites of the period were mostly excavated in the last century, and there have been few recent excavations to give a clearly documented story. Although wheelhouses were not built in Orkney, the sequence of events there is similar to that in Shetland, and the post-broch pottery from the Orcadian sites tallies favourably with that of the wheelhouse period at Jarlshof.

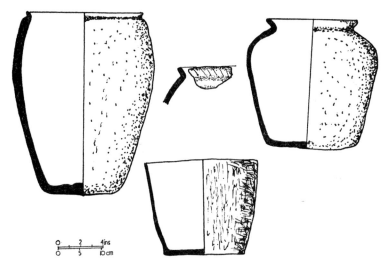

Fig 46   Wheelhouse pottery, Jarlshof

THE PICTS

The Picts have become one of the romantic mysteries of early Christian Britain, largely because the documentary and archaeological evidence for them is tantalisingly inadequate. But because the Picts are sparsely documented now, it does not mean that they were any more barbarous or less literate than their contemporaries; indeed, there is good reason to suppose that they kept as detailed records as their neighbours. Original documents which date from before AD 850 are relatively rare, and what survives does so mainly through transcription at a later date in the Middle Ages. Pictish, which ceased to exist as an official language after the accession of Kenneth Mac Alpin in the ninth century, would have been beyond the comprehension of medieval copyists. This would not explain why their Latin writings were not copied (for it can be presumed that Latin was largely used in official Pictish documents)—it is possible that some were, but have been lost as a result of the Edwardian campaigns in Scotland, the destruction of cathedral records at the time of the Scottish Reformation, or possibly at the time of the Viking raids. Whatever the cause may have been, not a single sentence of the language has survived in a document, and our sources of Pictish are a few brief inscriptions in Pictish ogham script, a couple of inscriptions in Latin letters, and a number of placenames and personal names. From this however it has proved possible to establish certain facts about the Picts and their language.

Basically, Pictish appears to have been related to the form of Celtic that was spoken in Wales, Cornwall and Cumbria. The Celtic element however in Pictish is earlier than Old Welsh, and has certain affinities with Gaulish, the language of the continental Celts. Pictish seems to have been by no means a pure Celtic language, and one can detect a much earlier substratum which belongs to a pre-Celtic and probably non Indo-European tongue. This old element was probably the language of the Bronze Age natives of north-east Scotland and must have been very strong, indicating an important indigenous Bronze Age element in the population who were the ancestors of the Picts.

This picture of the origins of the Picts connects well with what is known of the Abernethy culture. This developed on the north-east mainland of Scotland out of the native late Bronze Age as a result of new contacts with northern Europe. These new contacts, which brought timber-laced forts, new pottery types and bronze objects, could easily have introduced the Celtic element in the language. The Picts in fact seem to have developed out of the Abernethy culture, and in the early centuries AD we can probably recognise the ancestors of the historic Picts in the tribes referred to by Roman writers as living in the east Highlands, notably the Maeatae and Caledonii. By the fourth century the Picts are a historical phenomenon, and are mentioned as taking part along with the Scots of Ireland and others in a great raid in AD 367 on the northern frontiers of Roman Britain. The twofold division of the proto-Picts into Caledonii and Maeatae may have continued into historic times, for the historian Bede speaks about the Northern Picts and Southern Picts, though this may merely have been for the purposes of convenience.

The name 'Pict' itself is curious. It appears in classical writings towards the end of the third century. It has often been taken to mean 'painted' and to allude to the Pictish custom of tattooing. The native name for them was *Cruithni*.

Pictish history begins with Bridei mac Maelcon, who reigned sometime in the second half of the sixth century. He won a decisive victory over King Gabran of the Scots (who occupied Argyll) and fifteen years peace between Picts and Scots seems to have followed. Bridei figures prominently in Scottish tradition as King Brude of the Picts, who was converted to Christianity by Columcille (Columba). A conventional account of this is given by Adomnan, Columcille's biographer. The full extent of Bridei's kingdom is unknown, though it probably included Orkney, since the sub-king or *regulus* of Orkney was at Bridei's court in the time of Columcille.

Orkney is mentioned again in documents around the year 574, when Aidan mac Gabran became king of Dalriada. It seems likely that around this time Orkney was in rebellion against its Pictish overlords, for we hear of Aidan campaigning in Orkney and encroaching on a part of southern Pictland. At its greatest extent Pictland stretched over the whole of northern Scotland beyond the Forth-Clyde line, except for that part of western Scotland and the Western Isles under the Dalriadic Scots. Most of Pictish history is concerned with the wars between the Picts and Scots and, later, between the Picts and the Angles of Northumbria. The Picts disappear from history around 850, when Kenneth Mac Alpin of the Scots became the first king of both Picts and Scots.

The extent to which the Northern Isles were Pictish at any given time is difficult to assess. Certainly they are outside the primary area of the Picts. There is however a strong tradition, as evidenced by early medieval historians, that Orkney came under them. Even earlier, at the turn of the fourth century, the Roman historian Claudian referred to the Picts in Shetland.

It is perhaps significant in this connection that almost half the Pictish ogham inscriptions in Scotland come from the Northern Isles, and Shetland has produced more than any other Scottish county. Pictish oghams date from the eighth century, the ogham script being a type of alphabet devised in Ireland based on transverse lines along a main stem. The early Irish used ogham for memorial stones for the dead, imitating the style of late or sub-Roman tombstones. The Picts probably acquired the alphabet from the Scots of Dalriada as a result of their campaigns. The abundance of Pictish oghams in the Northern Isles is the outcome not only of a strong Pictish element in the population, but also of Irish. The name 'Nechton' (Nehhton) appears on a stone from Lunnasting, Shetland, while the Scottish (ie Irish) element is suggested by 'meqq' (which is related to the Irish *maqqi*, meaning 'son of') on the Bressay Stone or 'crosscc' (a version of the Irish name for 'cross') also on the Bressay Stone. The Irish element was probably supplied by Irish clerics—the *papae*—who have given their name to many placenames in the Northern Isles, such as Papil.

In an interesting account set down around 1200 by a Norse writer in Orkney, we are informed that the Orkneys were first inhabited by Picts (*Peti*) and Irish-Scottish priests (*papae*), and that the Picts were little more than pygmies who did wonders in the morning and evening, building towns, but at midday completely lost their strength and hid themselves in underground houses. It also tells us that the Orkneys were called Pictland (*terra Petorum*) and that the papae were so called on account of their white robes. The reference to underground houses is particularly significant in view of the Passage House of the final pre-Norse phase at Jarlshof or less relevantly, the souterrains of Orkney.

Some Scandinavian placenames in the Northern Isles incorporate elements implying the presence of Picts, such as Pettadale (valley of the Picts), Petester (homestead of a Pict) or Pettafell (mountain of the Picts), while the Pentland Firth itself means 'firth land of the Picts'. It might seem strange that no obviously Pictish names survive in the Northern Isles. This need not however surprise us, since most would have been lost beneath the heavy overlay of Norse in subsequent centuries.

In all probability, then, the inhabitants of the Northern Isles in the period prior to the Norse colonisation were under Pictish control, and it is probably legitimate to speak of the post-broch cultures of the Northern Isles as being Pictish, while the broch builders may be called proto-Picts.

Pictish art

There is very little archaeological evidence for the Picts apart from their art. They were skilled metalworkers, but except for the St Ninian's Isle treasure and a few isolated pieces, little of their metalwork has survived, and their art is best seen in the important and unique series of sculptured stones that they produced. The earliest of these are the Class I symbol stones—simple undressed stones decorated with incised symbols. Class II stones are somewhat later and consist of dressed slabs of varying dimensions with sculpture in relief. There is a cross on one side of these stones, decorated with interlace and frequently with subsidiary motifs. On the other face are found Pictish symbols in relief, often combined with other detail.

The symbols that appear on the stones fall into two categories:

animals, almost all of which could have been found in Pictland at the time the stones were carved; and other symbols, some of which such as a mirror, a comb or a sword are recognisable objects, but the remainder of which are puzzling abstract designs. Of the animals, the only creature that would have been unknown to the Picts was that called the 'Pictish beast' or 'swimming elephant', a mythical creature that was probably developed out of a type of S-shaped dragon popular in Romano-British art (Fig 47).

It has been pointed out that the animals are carved with naturalism and a great economy of line, also with a number of distinctive conventions such as the use of a spiral to indicate the shoulder muscle. These characteristics are shared by a widespread tradition of animal art which occurs among the nomads of the steppes and which seems to have been developed by them, though it was transmitted even as far as Persia and China and occurs in various forms at widely separated dates. It has been suggested that this 'Eurasiatic' animal art was transmitted from the steppe land to Europe in the early Iron Age, and from there came to Scotland with migrants from England shortly before the coming of the Romans. While this is an attractive theory, there is one serious obstacle in the way of its acceptance—there are almost no examples of Eurasiatic animal art along the supposed line of its transmission, and although there are animals in the Iron Age art of Scotland they are not really very similar to their supposed Pictish descendants. This has been explained by the suggestion that the animal art was confined to perishable materials such as leather or textiles, or more probably body tattoos. At present the origin of the Pictish animals must therefore remain a mystery, though it is quite possible that the Eurasiatic animal style was one of the many art styles current in Europe at the time of the folk movements of the post-Roman 'migration period' and animals related to the Pictish elsewhere in Britain date from the early Christian period. The inanimate symbols are even more puzzling, for while it can again be argued that many appear to be representations of things familiar in Iron Age Scotland but not known to the historical Picts, it can equally well be argued that the repre-

Fig 47 *Pictish symbols (after Henderson)*

sentations are not sufficiently distinctive for this to be certain, and some of the objects at least would have been familiar in the fifth or sixth centuries AD.

The symbols appear repeatedly with little variation in the form, in a variety of combinations. There can be little doubt that the combination of symbols is intentional, and that they are meant to convey a message. What this message is remains a puzzle, but there are two possible explanations. The first is that they are memorial stones, the animal symbols being perhaps clan badges, and the inanimate symbols being indicators of personal rank. Unfortunately only one, from Birsay in Orkney, has actually been associated with a grave, and the precise nature of that association is not certain. The alternative explanation is that they are marks of ownership, used in pre-Christian times to define private land boundaries and in Christian times to denote the extent of church possessions. The remarkable uniformity of the symbols suggests that they did not merely evolve but were developed at one point in time deliberately, perhaps by a single person.

The custom of erecting symbol stones probably started on the north mainland, round the Moray and Dornoch Firths, where the most carefully executed and stylistically early examples occur. At a later date they spread throughout Pictland. They may span a comparatively long time. The dating evidence is problematic, but Pictish symbols appear on silverwork from a hoard found at Norrie's Law, Fife, which has been dated by a Byzantine coin and Roman hack silver to the late sixth century. At the opposite end of the scale, a number of Class I stones have Pictish ogham inscriptions. While these may, in some cases at least, be later than the symbols, it would suggest that the stones themselves were still meaningful in the eighth century AD.

There are quite a number of Pictish symbol stones from the Northern Isles. From Redland, in Orkney, comes a stone with a 'rectangle' and a 'crescent and V-rod'; from St Peter's Church on South Ronaldsay another incomplete stone, while yet others come from Greens, Mainland and Knowe of Burrian near Loch Harray. Apart from these, and the stone already mentioned from Birsay which

11a The Brough of Deerness, Orkney, early Christian monastery
11b Brough of Birsay, Orkney: ecclesiastical complex with Norse house in foreground

12   Buckquoy, Birsay, Orkney: Dark Age hut

belongs rather to Class II, a phalange bone of an ox was found in the secondary occupation levels at the Broch of Burrian, incised with a 'crescent and V-rod' on one side and a mirror case on the other. Burrian also produced a stone with some unusual and indeterminate engravings, while another broch, Oxtro, produced a slab engraved with an eagle in Pictish style which had been used as a covering slab for a cist (Fig 48). Shetland has produced far fewer recognisable Pictish symbols; they appeared on a stone from Sandness now lost but drawn, fortunately, in the eighteenth century, and on a sandstone disc from Jarlshof, which bears a 'double disc and Z-rod'. A number of other stones have engravings in the Pictish tradition, but not of orthodox Pictish symbols (Pl 10a).

Pictish settlements

Very little is known about the nature of the settlements of the Picts in Orkney, though it can be assumed with some degree of safety that the wheelhouses of Shetland were occupied and built by the historical Picts. In Orkney evidence comes primarily from the post-broch occupation levels of some brochs. It has been mentioned that Pictish symbol engravings have come from the Broch of Burrian and the Broch of Oxtro; the former also produced a Celtic ecclesiastical bell of the early Christian period. Unfortunately these two sites were both excavated in the last century, as was Lingro, another broch with extensive post-broch occupation.

More information is available from the two brochs in Orkney excavated this century—Aikerness and Midhowe. At Midhowe small chambers were constructed outside the broch, and in one case the broch wall was actually cut away to a depth of about 5ft. The ditch was also partly filled in. At Aikerness a vast complex of secondary huts was built round the broch, often with a central hearth and generally of roughly circular shape. These have produced, apart from pottery akin to the wheelhouse wares, a number of objects of fifth/sixth-century date, most notably a fine bronze penannular brooch.

Another site occupied in this period is Buckquoy, Birsay (Pl 12).

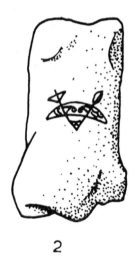

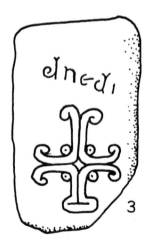

Fig 48   Pictish (1) and early Christian (3) stones, Orkney, and
          (2) Pictish inscribed bone
          (1) Ronaldsay
          (2) Broch of Burrian
          (3) St Nicholas Chapel, Papa Stronsay

Here below three successive Norse houses was found a sub-rectangular hall leading to a circular chamber. This in turn replaced an earlier rectilinear structure built of upright slabs, which was found incomplete due to stone robbing. This is the first instance of a rectangular building in the Northern Isles; the plan could easily have been introduced by the Picts, who were certainly in the habit of building rectangular structures, if we can judge by the Pictish timber hall built at Clatchard's Craig in Fife. It could also have been partly due to the influence of the Irish clerics, and indeed a monastery of rectangular cells is known at Deerness. At Skaill, Deerness, the excavations at present in progress have produced pottery closely related to the type of wheelhouse pottery found at Jarlshof, but as yet no structures.

The most distinctive and abundant finds of this period consist of pins of bone and bronze used as dress fasteners. Many show affinities to late Roman pins, and are probably derived from them, while a few are similar to types found in Ireland in the early Christian period. Yet others appear to be of types peculiar to Scotland though not, as far as can be established, to Pictland (Fig 49). From Birsay comes one of the best Pictish objects found in Scotland—a fine wooden box, about 12in long and dating from the eighth century or slightly later. It was found containing tools, probably those of a wood carver and metalworker, or possibly a leatherworker. It is adorned with abstract decoration, the basic motif being running scrolls.

Pictish metalwork

Until the discovery of the St Ninian's Isle treasure in 1958, it was not fully realised that there was a thriving tradition of metalworking in Pictland producing works comparable in their beauty to the Irish. The St Ninian's Isle hoard has however led to the recognition of other works, the most notable of which is the Monymusk reliquary, a seventh-century shrine traditionally associated with St Columcille. Most of the early examples of Pictish metalwork that have survived come from southern Pictland or are stray objects from further south; they include the silver objects from Norrie's Law in Fife. The most

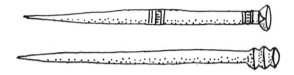

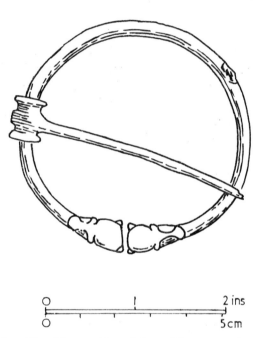

Fig 49   Pins from Ronaldsay and brooch from Aikerness, early Christian period

characteristic objects of this period are massive silver chains, intri-
cately woven, some of which bear Pictish symbols, and 'hand-pins', a
type of dress-fastener with a head slightly reminiscent of a partly
clenched fist which was also popular in Ireland. To the seventh and
eighth centuries belong a series of penannular brooches, of which
characteristic examples were found in the St Ninian's Isle Treasure.

The most typical have lobed terminals or terminals in the form of facing animal heads.

A Pictish metalworker's workshop was found at Birsay before World War II, but the information gained still remains unpublished. Here numerous clay moulds for penannular brooches and other objects were found, as well as other metalworking refuse. This workshop was probably in operation in the eighth century, and the finds from Birsay include part of a brooch that was miscast and thrown away.

Two other interesting finds of Pictish metalwork were also made in Orkney. One is a fragmentary bronze mount with two intertwining animals, the other is a wheel-shaped mount with roundels and squares with lobes reminiscent of Pictish penannular brooch terminals. The first was found at Monker Green, Stromness, the second with another decorated mount, a number of beads and a few other small objects at the Knowe of Moan, Loch Harray.

St Ninian's Isle Treasure (Pl 9). The St Ninian's Isle Treasure, found in excavations carried out by Aberdeen University on a church site on the tidal St Ninian's Isle, Shetland, is the most important discovery of metalwork of the early Christian period ever to be made in Scotland. Its importance in western and northern Britain is on a par with Sutton Hoo in English archaeology.

The hoard consisted of 7 silver bowls, one almost hemispherical, the others with omphaloid bases; 2 sword chapes; 3 objects shaped like pepper pots; a sword pommel; a spoon, a single-pronged claw-shaped object, possibly for eating shellfish; a hanging bowl; 12 penannular brooches and the jawbone of a porpoise. It was found in a wooden box made of larch, and had been buried under a cross-inscribed, broken sandstone slab near the chancel arch of a twelfth-century church. This church was the latest of a series of structures on the site, the earliest of which was Iron Age, and which also included an early Christian building. Seven post stones of a corner-post shrine, decorated with Pictish symbols, were among the other finds from the site.

Some of the objects in the hoard, such as the sword chapes, showed considerable wear, and there is good reason to suppose that not all are contemporary. In all probability the date of deposition was the late eighth or early ninth century, almost certainly in the face of a Norse invasion threat. No Viking would bury a hoard of loot on an ecclesiastical site in regular use, and the only other likely explanation is that it belonged to a Pictish chief. This is supported by the fact that one sword chape had a Pictish inscription

IN NOMINE D(EI) S(UMMI)
RESADF (or K) ILISPU (or B)SSCIO

Resad and Spusscio are personal names. The 'fili' meaning 'son of' appears as an inscription formula on a series of early Christian memorial stones, being the Latinisation of the Irish word 'maqq' which, as we have seen, appears in Pictish ogham inscriptions. The inscription and other factors indicate Pictland as the most likely provenance for the whole hoard, except perhaps the hanging bowl, which may be Northumbrian. Although claims have been made that it is ecclesiastical, it is almost certainly a secular treasure.

Punched dots adorn the bowls; in four cases this takes the form of interlace or rectilinear patterns, in two there is a frieze of animals. An internal mount on the base of the smallest bowl is inlaid with red enamel, while the hemispherical bowl has complex geometric decoration of incised lines bordered with punched dots in a series of curves. The hanging bowl has three ribs in the form of boars. In the centre of the base there is a roundel with animal ornament, with a circular disc in the same position on the exterior. The sword chapes are decorated with animal ornament and blue glass studs, while the 'pepper pots' which may be buttons or belt fasteners, are decorated in a similar style. The spoon and the pronged implement have loops for suspension, and the spoon is adorned with a dog's head at the base of the stem, which appears to lick from the bowl. The twelve penannular brooches are, with one exception, gilt on one face. They belong to two main classes, those with lobed terminals and those with plate terminals. All are decorated with carved interlace and occasional animal motifs.

The bowls and brooches are the most distinctively Pictish objects in the hoard. The animals on some of the bowls compare favourably with those on some of the later Class II Pictish stones, while the brooches belong to a general class whose distribution is confined, except for a few outliers, to north-east Scotland.

Some objects in the hoard show other influences, notably from manuscript art. This is particularly so in the case of the three 'pepper pots', which have decoration paralleled in the famous Book of Kells, which was executed, probably on Iona, around 800. The hanging bowl is of Anglo-Saxon workmanship, and was probably made in Northumbria in the late seventh or early eighth century. It was already old when the hoard was buried.

THE COMING OF CHRISTIANITY

At this point it is convenient to consider the archaeological evidence for early Christianity in the Northern Isles.

Christianity in Britain was in part a survival from Roman Britain, in part a reintroduction from the Mediterranean world. It is now generally held that little Christianity survived the upheavals that accompanied the withdrawal of the Roman forces and the Anglo-Saxon and other barbarian settlements of the fourth and fifth centuries. A few Christian enclaves may have remained—it seems likely that there was one in south-west Scotland centred on Whithorn, for example, for Ninian is almost certain to have gone from his seat at Carlisle to serve an already Christian community, and indeed archaeological evidence would seem to substantiate this. Another may have existed in south Wales. What is quite apparent however is that, contrary to tradition, there was no exodus of Christians to Wales, north Britain and south-west England following the coming of the Anglo-Saxon settlers. The evidence of the formulae used on early Christian memorial stones, together with other factors such as the distribution of imported Mediterranean pottery which seems initially to have been brought to western Britain and Ireland for liturgical use (though later it found its way to secular tables), suggests that Christianity in western Britain at any rate was mainly a reintroduction from the Mediterranean in the fifth and sixth centuries.

In southern Scotland the organisation of Christianity seems to have been diocesan, as it must have been in Roman Britain. The picture provided by archaeological evidence points to a spread of Christianity from the Whithorn-Carlisle region slowly northwards in the period from AD 400–600. By 600, if not before, four dioceses can be recognised in the Lowlands, centred on Carlisle, Whithorn, Glasgow and possibly Abercorn and Old Melrose. Carlisle and Whithorn probably belonged to the single diocese of Rheged, Glasgow to Strathclyde, Abercorn to Gododdin and Old Melrose to Greater Tweed-dale. Ninian and his successors were probably not missionary saints in the accepted sense, but responsible for conversion amongst ruling families. A tradition says that Ninian was responsible for the conversion of the Southern Picts, and certainly early Christian cemeteries with burials in long stone cists appear on both sides of the Forth. In the same way Columcille probably came to Iona in the first place to minister to an already Christian community in Argyll—the Dalriadic Scots. His missionary activity among the Picts was probably a secondary activity again conducted at a high level.

Whether or not Christianity reached the Southern Picts in the time of Ninian, it does not seem to have been well established in Pictland before the time of Columcille, and all earlier traces of it were absorbed with the establishment of the Columban church. The date of this is open to debate. Bede's date for the event is 565, but there are some grounds for rejecting his account and putting the date any time during Columcille's ministry at Iona. Certainly the work he initiated seems to have been effective, for Adomnan, Columcille's biographer, was able to write towards the end of the seventh century that Dalriada and the kingdom of the Picts escaped a plague due to 'Saint Columba, whose monasteries placed within the boundaries of both peoples, are down to the present time held in great honour by them both'. Thirty years later Bede was able to say of Iona that its 'monastery was for a long time the chief of almost all those of the Northern Scots, and all those of the Picts, and had the direction of their people'. It is quite probable that the conversion of the Northern Isles began as early as the time of Columcille, for Adomnan says

> On another occasion Cormac, the soldier of Christ . . . was seeking, for a second time, to find a hermitage in the ocean; leaving land, he had pressed on for many days, at full sail, across the boundless sea. St. Columba, who was staying beyond Druimalban, commended him to Brude, the king, in the presence of the sub-king of the Orkneys, saying: 'Some of our people have already set sail, desiring to find a hermitage in the untravelled ocean; if they, by any chance, should come, after a long journey, to the islands of Orkney, commend them earnestly to this sub-king, whose hostages are in your power, so that no harm may befall them at his hands'. The saint spoke in this manner because he knew in spirit that the same Cormac would come, after many months, to Orkney. And so it happened, and, by reason of the aforesaid commendation of the holy man, he was saved from sudden death in the Orkneys.

The importance of this passage lies in its implication that in the last quarter of the sixth century Orkney was still pagan. Conversion seems to have taken place during the seventh century, Shetland being converted as an extension. This hypothesis seems to be substantiated by the archaeological evidence. The early Christian memorial stones from the Northern Isles are Pictish, rather than Irish, in type, and the general character of the evidence for early Christianity in the Northern Isles suggests that the strongest influence came from Pictland and Northumbria rather than Ireland. While early church dedications are notoriously unreliable as evidence, it is significant perhaps that in the Northern Isles dedications are to British rather than Irish saints.

Probably the expulsion of Irish monks of Iona from Pictland, following the re-orientation of the Pictish church with Northumbria at the start of the eighth century had repercussions in Orkney and Shetland, with the establishment of further contacts with Northumbria and thence the Gregorian church.

Chapel sites

The simplest type of early Christian site in the British Isles is the undeveloped cemetery—this can be enclosed or open. Open cemeteries are rare, though many of the long-cist cemeteries of Scotland are of the unenclosed, undeveloped types. Where cemeteries are bounded by an enclosure this is usually circular or oval in plan, being demarcated by a low bank. The circular shape is particularly interesting, for it would appear that it represents a survival of the long tradition of circular ritual enclosures in Britain, starting with Neolithic and Beaker henges of the type encountered in Orkney, through the many types of funerary barrow (including many classes of chambered tomb) to circular Romano-Celtic temples. In this connection it is interesting that many pre-Christian sites seem to have been re-used as early Christian burial grounds. To cite but one example, in the Catstane cemetery at Kirkliston, near Edinburgh, the long-cist cemetery of inhumation burials within a circular enclosure seems to have been preceded by a short-cist burial with a cremation. This recurring manifestation of the sacred circle is probably due to the immediately apparent symbolism of the barrier separating the holy from the profane or, in cemeteries, the dead from the living.

The undeveloped cemetery is the earliest and simplest form of ecclesiastical site. A developed cemetery is one in which there are special graves, usually of revered personages, which are demarcated in one of several ways, or one in which there are timber chapels or oratories, square emplacements called *leachta* (see p 154) or other structures.

Early chapels and oratories were built of wood, and in a few cases these have been excavated, as at Ardwall Island in Galloway, Church Island in County Kerry or at Burryholms off the coast of Wales. Stone chapels do not appear until the late seventh and eighth centuries AD, and like their timber predecessors were usually unicameral buildings of unpretentious appearance, built with the side to end walls in a 2:3 ratio, not infrequently 15ft by 10ft internally. The changeover from wood to stone which, incidentally, is reflected in a transition from erecting wooden crosses to stone ones, is probably due to a changing function—the wooden oratories were intended to accommodate one or two bretheren alone, while the stone churches ministered also to a lay congregation.

It is often very difficult to determine without excavation whether the remains of simple stone churches that are visible inside circular graveyards belong in fact to the early Christian period or whether they are Medieval: very probably the majority of visible remains of chapel sites in the Northern Isles are Medieval, but stand on the sites of early Christian foundations. The discovery of early Christian stones on the site, or sometimes Viking-period hoards, can hint at early Christian predecessors.

Monasticism (Fig 50)

Monasticism was introduced to south-west Britain from the Mediterranean in the later fifth century. In the sixth century, impetus was added to the movement in Britain from Gaul, Aquitaine and southern Spain. The first monastic sites in Britain antedate 500 and are in the South-West and Wales; by the later sixth century they can be traced in Ireland and Northumbria. Monks were probably to be found in fifth-century Britain and Ireland, but the monastery in the sense of the permanent enclosed community with dependant hermitages, education and obedience to a Rule are a later phenomenon.

The form of early Christian monasteries was quite different from the complexes that are associated with the term from acquaintance with medieval abbeys. In the early Christian period there was no careful layout of buildings round a cloister, instead, a scatter of buildings within an earthen rampart—the *vallum monasterii*—which, in contrast to the graveyards of the period, was usually rectangular or square. In a few cases the rampart may have been built of stone. This concept of a rectangular enclosure was new to Britain, and originated in the East,

Fig 50   Deerness (after R.C.H.A.M.S.)

where the earliest permanent monastic establishments are to be found. These were usually enclosed by a stone wall, often of considerable height, as they frequently had to serve, especially in the desert, as fortresses against hostile tribes. While in Britain and Ireland there is no known case of an early Christian monastery being garrisoned against attack, many are sited within earlier forts, possibly because the land on which they were built was a gift from a local chieftain. Islands too were popular. The monastic complex on Birsay in Orkney and on Papil on West Burra in Shetland are comparable examples, both with rectilinear enclosures.

Alongside the large, rectilinear monasteries were smaller foundations, often, like the graveyards, enclosed by circular or oval *valla*. A third class was the small eremitic monastery, located in remote places. These were no more than communal hermitages, where up to a dozen monks under the authority of an abbot lived in isolation. While the major monasteries had in some cases several chapels, many living cells and workshops, the smaller ones might consist simply of a chapel with a few small rectangular living cells or, very occasionally, circular 'beehive' cells.

Birsay (Fig 51). The most important of the Orkney monasteries was undoubtedly that on Birsay. Situated on a tidal island, now approached by a causeway, Birsay has produced both extensive Viking period and later remains and evidence of the pre-Norse Christian foundation. The surviving remains of the early period are not very substantial. They consist of a roughly built wall under the south wall of the nave of the twelfth-century church of St Mary. Contemporary with it, and underlying the Norse cemetery, is the fragmentary wall of a sub-rectangular enclosure, probably delimiting an area about 130ft across. Two cross slabs belong to the monastic cemetery, which consisted of long-cists of slate. The stumps of uninscribed headstones still survived for the excavator, though they would not have projected above the ground surface in Norse times. Towards the south wall of the enclosure was a burial with three cists, at the head of which was the shattered fragments of the Birsay stone. This stone has a Pictish eagle symbol in the upper register with a procession of three figures carrying curious square shields and spears below; presumably these figures represent the three Picts buried in the graves. Stylistically it probably should be assigned to the eighth century.

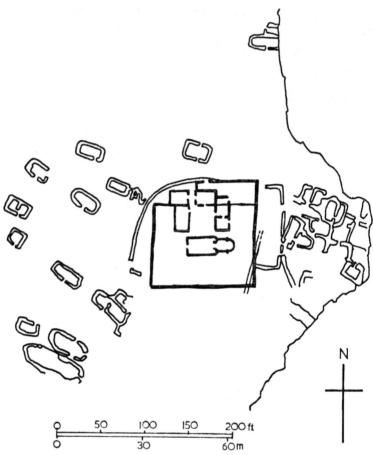

Fig 51 Birsay (after Cruden)

To the east of the grave was a badly preserved mound lined with a kerb some 10ft long, which the excavator has interpreted as a *leacht*. None of these curious square or rectangular constructions of stones or masonry blocks have been excavated: they probably mark graves, and are frequently still used in Ireland as the stations of penitential processions. The most famous site on which they occur is Inismurray in

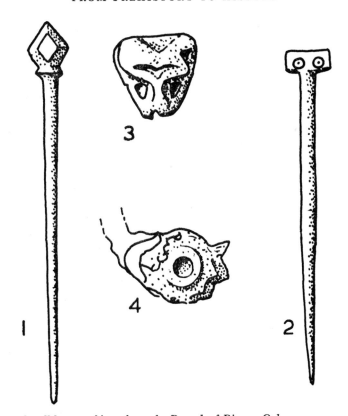

Fig 52 *Small bronze objects from the Brough of Birsay, Orkney*
     1, 2 Norse period pins   *3 Feline ornament*
     4   *Miscast 'waster' of the terminal of a Pictish penannular brooch*

Sligo. They were probably altars erected above a martyr's tomb or another special grave, round which various rites connected with the martyr cult were centred. The Irish word *leacht* is connected with the Latin *lectus* meaning a bed or grave. Whether or not all *leachta* stood above graves is a point for debate, and some may have been simply open-air altars.

Papil. The Shetland monastic site of comparable importance is Papil on West Burra. Here a substantial amount of rectilinear earthwork vallum survives beneath the modern churchyard wall. The present ruined church dates from 1815, but at the time of writing traces of earlier masonry were visible beneath the floor. To the west of the church is the platform of what is probably the medieval church and possibly another chapel. Immediately to the north a cross slab and the remains of two shrines were found, while to the south were found a tall cross slab and the so-called 'Papil Stone' (see p 160).

The Papil shrines are of particular interest. Records exist of a complete side panel (which still survives and is on display in Lerwick Museum), three short panels (lost), two corner posts each with a groove for a panel, a third one (lost), two corner posts with two grooves each and the top of another corner post. From this it has been deduced that one of the Papil shrines was a double one in the form of a large stone box, with side and end panels slotted into stone corner posts. A skull is reported to have been found in this double shrine. The other shrine was of similar type, but had no central dividing slab. These monuments are the final stage in a series of developments in early shrines, and the preceding stages are worth considering.

The custom of venerating relics seems to have reached Britain in the fifth century from the Mediterranean, where the shrine of St Peter appears to be the earliest example. The relics of the early Christians were of two types, corporeal and representative, the former being the bones or part of the body of a revered personage, the latter being either something which he wore or used, or something that had had extensive contact with him. When the cult of relics became established, it was customary for the remains of the saint to be disinterred—it could be after any length of time but five to ten years was common—and translated to a shrine. It was currently held that touching the relics was a cure for disease, though they were also held to disperse evil and to be capable of controlling natural events.

The first stage in the development of shrines for relics was the construction of special tombs for martyrs in a cemetery—little yards known as *cellae memoriae*—around which later churches were often

13 Silver objects from the Viking hoard from Skaill, Orkney

built. One early series of shrines is derived from a particular type of wooden superstructure above a grave known as a *totenmemoria*; this had a hipped roof, like a chapel in miniature, which was in turn the wooden copy of a ridge-lidded sarcophagus, representing a chapel. Stone versions of these structures are known from Scotland, from Jedburgh and St Andrews. Shrines like these were four-piece (excluding lids or roofs), whereas shrines of the Papil type were either eight-piece (in the case of single shrines) or thirteen-piece (in the case of the double), the side and end panels being slotted into stone posts or blocks. This arrangement has resulted in the term 'corner-post shrine' used to describe them.

Double shrines of the Papil type are probably Northumbrian in origin. Indeed, the corner-post shrine seems to be mainly a North British phenomenon, all the recorded examples coming from Scotland. In Ireland slab shrines (the 'roof' part of the shrine only) seem to have been the type favoured. Although no actual double shrine survives in Northumbria, Bede describes just such a double shrine of wood that was set up in Monkwearmouth in 716, to contain the skeletons of two previous abbots.

One of the side slabs from Papil shows a procession of five clerics in hooded capes, advancing towards a free-standing High Cross on a block base. Four are on foot, one on a pony, and they carry croziers and book satchels. Below them is a stylised running scroll design. The style of the cross is reminiscent of Northumbrian work, and it is possible that the scene is a depiction of the coming of Christianity to Shetland. It dates from the late eighth or early ninth century in all probability, and also shows Pictish influence. One of the Papil corner posts is also decorated, with an incised expanded terminal cross between two S-shaped motifs, and obviously projected above the level of the lid.

It has been argued quite convincingly that the slotted post-and-panel technique of the shrines is derived not from carpentry but from slotted post-and-panel chancel screens, which were probably introduced into Northumbria from ultimately Mediterranean sources in the late seventh century when Benedict Biscop first brought continental masons and carvers to work there. Probably the first stage was one in which the chancel screen was used to enclose the shrine, then at a second stage formed the shrine itself. Such shrines as these no doubt stood in churches.

Fragments of two other double shrines come from the excavations at St Ninian's Isle in Shetland, with knobbed corner posts several of which are decorated, one with Pictish symbols (Fig 53).

Apart from the shrines, the most famous of the other stones from Papil is the Papil Stone, which is decorated with a disc-headed cross, below the head of which are four crozier-carrying clerics, two with book satchels round their necks. A very spirited Pictish lion decorates the panel beneath, while below two puzzling bird-headed figures stand, axes over their shoulders and a human head between their beaks. The style of the figures would suggest a similar date for the Papil Shrine slab, though the decoration on the head of the cross seems earlier.

Three other notable stones from Papil are an interlaced cross, a socketed stone with an incised cross, and a simple incised cross.

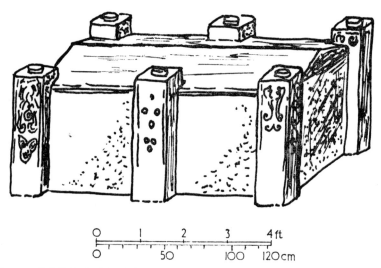

Fig 53   St Ninian's Isle shrine reconstruction (after Thomas)

Smaller monasteries. Apart from Birsay and Papil there are a number of smaller monasteries in the Northern Isles. The most famous of these is the Brough of Deerness, on the east Mainland of Orkney (Pl 11a). The monastery stands on an inaccessible headland. The complex is enclosed by a stone wall on the south (landward) side, with the other sides demarcated by the steep cliffs. The site was much damaged during World War II, but the complex consists of a rectangular oratory measuring internally 17ft by 9¾ft, with walls bedded in clay, surrounded by a complex of rectangular buildings, the largest of which is about 40ft by 27ft externally. There are also a few circular huts. It is reminiscent of Tintagel, but is probably later, possibly belonging to the eighth century.

A smaller site is Munkerhouse on Papa Westray. Although nothing is now visible, a group of huts is said to underly the twelfth-century church and churchyard. The site has produced a cross slab of the early Christian period and a Norse hogback stone.

In Shetland, a comparable site is Lunna, on Mainland, where the remains are difficult to assess. The vallum where it is preserved stands to a height of about 4ft in places, and encloses a sub-rectangular area some 40yd in diameter. It has within it a unicameral stone church and a curious long building with an apsidal end, some 55ft by 11ft. There are other indeterminate remains of buildings.

Three eremitic monasteries in Shetland are now almost inaccessible except by helicopter but have recently been planned for the first time and are worthy of mention. One is at Birrier, on Yell, once reached by a land-bridge that is now badly denuded. As at Deerness, there is a stone vallum on the landward side, behind which are fourteen rectangular buildings with slightly bowed sides and rounded corners. A similar site at Northmavine, Kame of Isbister, has nineteen buildings, though twenty-two were counted at one time. The third site, Outer Brough, is a rock stack off Fetlar, has sixteen stone buildings, again behind a stone wall on the landward side, one of which is larger and sub-divided.

CHAPTER 6

The Early Norse Period

THE COMING OF THE VIKINGS

The Viking as he is represented in modern literature and films is a bearded warrior in horned helmet who steps from his dragon-prowed ship intent on pillage, rape and arson. This image is partly the outcome of modern romanticism, but owes much to the saga-literature which traced the exploits of groups of Vikings and which was set down in Iceland in the eleventh century and later, when the culture which produced the Vikings was already waning. It was in the interests of the saga-writers to present their pagan ancestors as heroic adventurers, similarly it was in the interests of contemporary clerics in medieval Europe to represent the pagan raiders as a far greater menace than they probably were. After all, it was the clerics who were the chroniclers of their age, and it was clerics too who had most to fear from the Vikings since monasteries were the first objective of the plunderers. When Christianity embraced the Vikings they became a part of Europe, and therefore no longer a strange scourge to be feared by Christians. It is unlikely however that conversion greatly altered their character, and the *Orkneyinga Saga*, allowing for poetic licence, depicts the twelfth-century Norse in Orkney as being as savage as their eighth- and ninth-century ancestors.

To understand the Viking movements it is first necessary to appreciate that the Vikings themselves constituted only one element in the population of Scandinavia of the eighth to tenth centuries. Even the meaning of the term 'viking' itself is enigmatic, but can be taken to

Fig 54 Jarlshof

imply only the adventurers who left behind in Norway, Denmark and particularly Sweden a society of peaceful agriculturalists. The Scandinavia of the Age of the Vikings represents essentially an Iron Age society which had developed gradually during the immediately preceding centuries. Its rise can first be traced in Sweden, where in the sixth and seventh centuries there evolved a rich culture, notable for its artistic skills, which founded its wealth on trade. This trade was to remain important in later centuries in Sweden, and the Swedish expansion of the Viking period was more concerned with opening up trade routes to the East and round the Baltic than with raiding in northern and western Europe. The Swedes were particularly active in Russia, founding the towns of Novgorod and Kiev, and they were familiar in Byzantium and among the Arabs. The Danes, in contrast, seem to have been more concerned with northern Europe, and were to have their greatest impact on the England of King Alfred.

Of all the Scandinavians however the Norse were the most adventuresome, and it is the Norse who were the dominant element in the Scandinavian raids and subsequent settlements in Scotland. Beyond, they settled in Iceland and Greenland, and it is the Norse too who can claim to be the discoverers of North America. Although Norse, Danes and Swedes were clearly separate elements in the Viking raids, it is also clear that the raids and settlements in any given area were not usually entirely composed of people from the same homeland. In Orkney, for example, placenames show that although almost all the settlers were Norse there were also some Danes in the population. It is often difficult to distinguish the origins of particular groups of Vikings from contemporary chronicles, for chroniclers frequently called them simply Norse or Vikings, just as the term 'Norseman' is often used today with similar disregard for origins.

It is clear that the motives behind the Viking raids were multifarious. Pirate raids in order to obtain plunder was certainly one cause, but commercial expansion was probably another, for the Scandinavians were great traders and did not always obtain merchandise by irregular means. Climatic changes and possibly improved farming may have resulted in a considerable population explosion in Scandinavia in the eighth century, with inadequate farmland to support the increase. Such a situation would have given rise to the need for colonisation, a situation worsened by Scandinavian laws of primogeniture which left younger sons disinherited. The population expansion and dissatisfaction among the landless no doubt also gave rise to political tensions, and some raids at least must be seen as preludes to colonising ventures and as the result of squabbles and exile from the homeland. Probably there was no one cause for a Viking expedition, but a combination of factors leading to a seafaring adventure. In the Viking period as a whole however it is possible to detect a gradual shift in emphasis from 'tip and run' raids to colonisation and mercantile expeditions. Colonisation certainly seems to have been an important factor in the Scottish raids, but in England and France the Vikings seem to have been more intent on extracting taxes (*danegeld*) than on settling.

The Norse in Scotland

The Viking legacy to later medieval Europe was negligible, but it was not so in the Northern or Western Isles of Scotland. For Orkney, and to a lesser extent Shetland, the Age of the Vikings was indeed Golden, when for a while these islands in the far north of Britain were in the mainstream of European affairs. The Norse era in Scotland was far to outlive the period of Viking activity in the rest of Europe, and the Northern Isles were to remain a Norwegian (later Danish) possession down to the fifteenth century. Today they are still oriented to Scandinavia, and they still inherit such curious legal anomalies as the right to fish with a net in Shetland rivers. The dialect of an Orcadian from the more northerly isles is more readily intelligible to a Norwegian than to a Scottish mainlander.

The first Viking attacks on Britain appear to have been in the late eighth century, and may well have been a sequel to the first landings in the Northern Isles. In 793 there was an undoubted attack on Lindisfarne, followed the next year by a similar attack on Jarrow which was repulsed. Probably Scottish monasteries suffered similar raids to the

Northumbrian not long after—there are records of Iona being sacked in the early ninth century. It seems clear that Orkney and Shetland were settled before the end of the ninth century, Orkney becoming a Norse earldom subject to the King of Norway. By the eleventh century the power of the Norse Orkney leader, Earl Thorfinn the Mighty, extended to Shetland, the Western Isles and nine Scottish earldoms.

During the Norse period, not only the Northern Isles, but also the north mainland of Scotland and the Hebrides had a dominant Norse population. The Hebrides were however more closely related to Ireland and Iceland, and indeed were also linked with the Isle of Man in the Kingdom of Man and the Isles. Many important Icelandic families seem to have had Hebridean origins, and for this reason the Western Isles are well documented in Icelandic sources. The Viking expansion to the Western Isles certainly appears to have taken place at an early date, in the late eighth or early ninth century, and an eighth-century Viking grave is recorded from Lamlash on Arran. The traditional story of the settlement of the Hebrides is given in the *Eyrbygja Saga,* which narrates how Ketill Flatnose became first Norse ruler of the Hebrides sometime before the mid-ninth century. Lewis was probably entirely Norse speaking in the eleventh century, and there is evidence to suppose that the Norse of the Western Isles were very wealthy—finds from Viking ship burials in the area are particularly fine. Norse placenames indicate the extent of Norse settlement; they occur throughout the Western Isles, the west mainland including Kintyre, and Arran.

In the extreme south-west the Norse penetrated Galloway and settled round the Solway in the early tenth century. This settlement can be associated with the establishment of the Norse kingdom of Dublin, and placenames attesting their presence are hybrid Irish-Norse forms. The settlers were in part at least Christian, though one grave find is pagan in character and there are possible ship burials in Galloway.

The evidence for the Northern Isles
The period of Norse domination in the Northern Isles can conveniently be divided into two periods, Pagan and Christian (see p 191).

The former extends from the later eighth century until the time of Earl Thorfinn the Mighty, who died about 1065, and it is with this period that we are primarily concerned in this chapter.

Although potentially there is abundant archaeological evidence in the Northern Isles, particularly Orkney, for the pagan Norse, it has never been adequately examined or collated. Jarlshof remains the only extensive settlement excavated and fully published in accordance with modern standards. In the last century some excavation was done at Orphir in Orkney, but apart from a few foundations outside the churchyard nothing is visible and very little is known, though the settlement associated with these buildings is known to be very extensive, covering an area at least as large as that of Jarlshof. Details of the Norse houses at Aikerness excavated by J. S. Richardson before World War II were unpublished on his death, and the only recent excavation of a house site to be published is that of Underhoull on Unst in Shetland. Work has however recently been carried out, notably at Skaill near Deerness on Orkney Mainland and at Buckquoy on Mainland opposite the tidal island at Birsay, and excavations have also yielded important results at Westness on Rousay. Likewise, apart from Aikerness the only Norse burials to be excavated since World War II are those at Westness and Buckquoy, and the accounts of earlier discoveries are often inadequate or confused. Yet many potential Norse sites, both of settlements and burials, are known, and it is quite certain many more still await mapping or recognition.

First Norse arrival in the Northern Isles (Fig 55)

The date of the first Norse *landnam* in the Northern Isles has been greatly debated, but generally today a date around 800 is favoured, though it is just possible that there were a few settlers in the ten years or so prior to that date, one grave from Skaill having a spearhead of a type current in eighth-century Scandinavia.

The evidence for the arrival of the Norse consists of documentary sources, most notably saga literature, placename evidence, and archaeological findings. Accurate dating for the latter is very difficult,

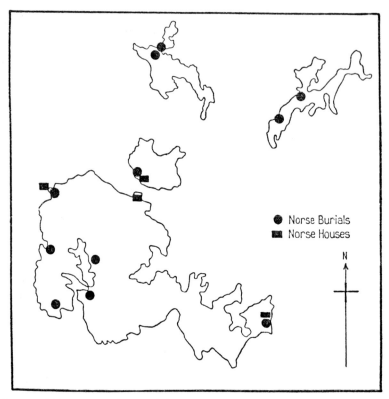

Fig 55   Viking sites in Orkney (after Radford)

though it can be said with confidence that most of the pagan graves from the Northern Isles belong to the period 800 to 850, to which period also belongs the first settlement at Jarlshof, the house at Underhoull, and possibly the first occupation at Birsay.

The date that is suggested by the Viking sagas is far removed from that implied by other evidence. The traditional story is given in the *Heimskringla*, a collection of royal sagas which tells how Harald Fairhair attempted to dominate the whole of Norway, with the result that many Norse fled to the Atlantic islands and set up headquarters from which to make raids on Harald's territory. Harald, according to the sagas, secured his position in Norway at the battle of Hafrsfjord, and then went on expeditions to destroy the nests of resistance in Shetland, Orkney, the Hebrides and finally the Isle of Man, setting up a client earldom in the Northern Isles under Ragnald, who in turn gave them to his brother Sigurd, who became the first earl of the Northern Isles. The same story is given in the *Orkneyinga Saga*. The date that the saga writers give for the battle of Hafrsfjord is 872, and if this were correct it would imply that the first settlement of the Northern Isles dates from this time. Current opinion now believes that the battle took place at a date nearer 900, which would render the picture given by the sagas even more at variance with the other evidence.

The reference to Viking raids in Britain in contemporary annals are more helpful as regards attempts to arrive at a date for the first Norse in the Northern Isles. Sources like the *Anglo-Saxon Chronicle* and, more important, Irish annals like the *Annals of Ulster* indicate that the Scandinavians only began to make serious raids on Britain around the last decade of the eighth century, and we can probably infer from this that the Norse were at that time making raids on Orkney and Shetland, shortly before the period of settlement. How much earlier there had been raids in the Northern Isles is difficult to estimate in the absence of documentary or other evidence; it is possible that there were a few Scandinavian attacks earlier in the eighth century but it seems likely that they were of little consequence.

Placename evidence is of additional value. *Byr* names are the oldest Scandinavian placenames in the Northern Isles. They are found in Orkney, for example, and some have been claimed as antedating 800. Probably however the majority, if not all, post-date 800. The *byr* element means in Orkney a 'farm' and is related to the Danish place-name in England ending in -*by*, which means a hamlet. Examples of *byr* names in the Northern Isles include Houseby, Trenabie and Kirkaby. Placenames incorporating the elements *land*, *garth* and *bister*, which are derived from the Norse *land*, *gardr*, and *bolstadr* are also early, and refer to attractive farmland. These also antedate 900, and belong to the period of settlement in the ninth century. Most of the other Orkney and Shetland Norse placenames are of later origin.

Before going on to consider the archaeological evidence for the early Norse in the Northern Isles, mention should be made of the rarer but important documentary evidence and of the legacy of placenames.

The 'Orkneyinga Saga'

In Iceland in the early thirteenth century the *Orkneyinga Saga* was composed, a remarkable epic which gives an account of the history of the Norse earldom in Orkney, Shetland and Caithness in the period from about 900 to 1200. It is the main documentary source for the period it covers, and is unusual in that the compiler has incorporated into it all the elements usually found in Icelandic sagas, and has skilfully drawn together information from a very wide range of sources. This means that in the main the saga is factually accurate, though historical fact is sometimes embellished in the interests of literary effect, and non-historical material also finds a place in the narrative for the same reason, in keeping with traditions of medieval historiography. The elements of Icelandic sagas used by the compiler of the *Orkneyinga Saga* are the 'family sagas', which dealt with the history of a particular family or families and which tend to be literary rather than historical; the 'kings' sagas', which were generally historical accounts of the kings of Norway and Denmark; the 'sagas of olden time' and the 'lying sagas' which are almost entirely fictitious and, finally saints' lives or other ecclesiastical material. Taken as a whole, the *Orkneyinga Saga* is a unique and outstanding work.

Placenames

The placenames that the Norse left for posterity provide clues to their way of life. 'Bister' names have already been mentioned—the name occurs in such forms as Rennibister, Wasbister or Braebister. Also very common are *saetr* names, in the form of *setter* as in Grim-setter, Winksetter or Livister; the original element means a house or homestead. An element which is sometimes confused with *saetr* is *stadr* which means a site or farm settlement. It occurs in placenames which incorporate -*sta*, -*ster* or often, in Orkney, -*ston*. Examples are Girlsta or Unstan (which is sometimes called Onston). Other very common name-elements are -*quoy*, meaning a cattle enclosure, from the Norse *kvi*; *skaill*, from the Norse *skali* meaning a hut; *brough*, meaning a 'fort' and derived from *borg*; *geo*, meaning a ravine or cleft in the coastline, from *gja*; *wall* or *voe*, meaning a creek or bay, from *vagr*; and *wick*, from *vik*, meaning a bay or inlet. Examples of these are Buckquoy, Quoyness, Langskaill, Sumburgh, Burrafirth, Ramnageo, Kirkwall, Hamnavoe, Lerwick or Sandwick. Mention might also be made of placenames derived from the Norse *ey* meaning an island, such as Egilsay, Rousay, Huney, and the placenames ending in -*a* such as Mousa, Balta, Foula or Papa.

In all, there are hundreds of Scandinavian placename elements in the Northern Isles, and thousands of Scandinavian placenames. One estimate of 50,000 placenames of Scandinavian origin in Shetland is regarded by many as conservative, and it has been reckoned that about 99 per cent of all Orkney farm names are of Norse derivation.

Pagan Viking graves

Of the numerous burials of the pagan Norse excavated in the Northern Isles, the most important are those found in a cemetery at Pierowall on Westray in Orkney. Here, in an area near the modern village, known as the Links, storms blew away the sand during the nineteenth century to reveal at least sixteen graves. These were investigated between 1839 and 1862, but unfortunately were not carefully recorded with the result that it is now not always certain which objects were associated with which grave, a task further complicated by the dispersal of many of the finds into numerous nineteenth-century collections. All appear to date from the ninth century, though a sword from one grave may perhaps be eighth century in date and was presumably an heirloom when it was buried.

A curious feature of several of the Pierowall graves was the presence of horse burials. In one case, Grave 7, the headless skeleton of a man was found, with the thigh bones crossed. Adjoining it was the entire skeleton of a horse, on its belly, with its head pointing towards the sea. A dog's skeleton (or rather part of it) came from the same grave, as well as a bridle bit with one of its rings in the horse's mouth, a buckle, a small piece of iron possibly from a spearhead or small sword and some indeterminate pieces of iron and bone.

Tortoise brooches were recovered from many of the Pierowall graves. These brooches, characteristic of pagan Norse burials, are oval and domical, adorned with bosses and openwork decoration. Other finds were equally characteristic—bone combs and comb cases, shield bosses, swords, whetstones, beads, ringed pins (pins with loose rings through their heads), an axe, buckles and knives.

Apart from Viking finds the discoveries at Pierowall include a fine Celtic brooch, unfortunately not associated with any particular grave. This penannular brooch is of bronze, and is decorated with interlace. The frames survive on it for rivet heads, of which two are still in place. It was probably quite old when it found its way into the Norse grave, and was a product of native workmanship in Scotland.

Another Celtic brooch was found in a Viking grave at Westness on Rousay (Pl 10b). Like the Pierowall brooch it too was probably old when it was buried, having been made perhaps as much as a century previously. It is of silver with inset gold panels, which in turn are decorated with filigree work and granular ornament, of which the most notable motifs are two interlacing animals. It is one of the finest Celtic penannular brooches known, and can be classed along with the Hunterston brooch from Ayrshire and Irish examples like the Tara brooch. The Westness brooch which dates from around the mid-eighth century was, like the Pierowall brooch, a Scottish product, though the shape (which is pseudo-penannular) is more characteristic of Irish workshops.

The Westness brooch was found in 1963, and came from the grave of a young woman, buried with a newborn child. With them were laid two iron heckles, a pair of shears, a small knife, a sickle, a long comb, a bronze basin, a whalebone plaque, an iron weaving sword, an iron socket that may have belonged to it and some bronze mounts. Round her neck the lady had worn a necklace of different coloured beads. At her shoulders were a pair of tortoise brooches. She had also worn a fine gilt bronze plaque. Other burials had previously been excavated at Westness from 1826 onwards, but from these graves only one sword survives.

Following the discovery of the 1963 burial, a group of Scandinavian archaeologists began excavations on the site in 1968. The finds were not as spectacular, but were nevertheless notable. Another grave was found, which yielded evidence of *sute*, a custom known from Scandinavia and the Isle of Man, which involved killing a woman to accompany her man to the afterlife. Buildings of the Norse period were also excavated.

Almost opposite Westness on Orkney Mainland another grave was discovered in 1939 during the excavations at the Broch of Gurness, Aikerness. At Aikerness the post-broch settlement was succeeded by a Norse community, who established a settlement on the site in the tenth century. The remains of the older buildings were levelled, and a farmstead was built on the top. It was quite customary for the Vikings to bury their dead near settlements, and therefore it is not surprising that burials were encountered near buildings at both here and at Westness. The Aikerness burial was also of a woman, who had been laid in a stone cist. Such cist burials are unusual, but at Aikerness it may be explained by the difficult nature of the site, which due to extensive building and limited topsoil above the bedrock did not lend itself to a dug grave. With the woman was found a pair of tortoise brooches, one with the impression of finely woven wool on the back; a necklet of shells; an iron sickle and a knife with a wooden handle. Another cist burial is known from Skaill.

At Buckquoy, near Birsay, the excavations of 1970–1 showed that the post-broch settlement had been followed by three successive longhouses. Partly overlying these was a male burial, associated with a bronze ring-headed pin, an iron knife, a whetstone, a javelin head and a silver halfpenny of the Anglo-Saxon King Edmund (940–6).

Most of the excavated Viking graves from Orkney appear to have been dug graves, without surface indications of their presence. At Pierowall most were of this type, though a few were possibly inserted into earlier pre-existing mounds. One was probably a ship burial. No other ship burials have as yet been excavated in the Northern Isles, though a number of mounds have been identified as such. The most interesting series is on Sanday.

Very little evidence for Viking burial custom has come from Shetland. There are only two certain graves of Viking date, both of women. The first, from Clibberswick, Unst, produced a pair of tortoise brooches, a trefoil brooch and some objects which have since been lost. The second, also from Unst, produced a tortoise brooch and a circular bronze box. A few stray finds suggest other Viking graves—there is an axe head from Whiteness and beads from a bog at Hillswick, for example.

Viking hoards

The Vikings are frequently associated with hoards of silver treasure, and the Northern Isles have produced several such collections, including one of the finest from the British Isles.

Of the five found in Orkney, the most important and impressive is that from Skaill near Sandwick, which was found in a rabbit hole in 1858 (Pl 13). In all, it consisted of almost 15lb of silver, and was composed of 9 brooches, 14 necklets of twisted silver, 27 simpler armlets and an assortment of ingots and silver fragments. In addition the hoard included 18 whole or fragmentary coins. These comprised Anglo-Saxon and Danish issues of Aethelstan and 'St Peter of York', together with Samanid and Abbasid dirhems. The presence of Arab coins can be explained by the fact that during the Viking period such silver dirhems were flooding into Scandinavia and were circulating to a lesser extent elsewhere in Europe. One was found in excavations at Winchester in 1964.

15a   Scalloway Castle, Shetland
15b   Tankerness House, Kirkwall, Orkney

16 St Magnus' Cathedral and the Bishop's Palace, Kirkwall, Orkney

The brooches are penannular and of 'thistle' type, that is, they have terminals and pin heads shaped like thistles. One of them has fine animal ornamentation in Jellinge style, named after a silver cup found at Jellinge in Denmark on which was a characteristic example of it. The Jellinge style was in fact developed in Britain—the Skaill brooch has better Jellinge decoration than any examples from Denmark—and is characteristic of the early phase of Scandinavian settlement in Britain. The style was current from the end of the ninth century until c AD 1000 (Fig 56).

Fig 56   Ornament from Viking brooch, Skaill, Orkney

The few coins found in the hoards from the Northern Isles were not currency, for the Vikings did not use coins as such. Instead they regarded them as hack silver, and transactions were carried out by weighing silver for the appropriate amount. Silver rings may have served as ring money, acting both as rings and as a type of currency whose value depended on their weight. Folding balances are frequently found in pagan Viking graves for weighing hack metal. One such was found in a grave at Gigha in the Hebrides, while another came from the excavations at Aikerness. The idea of coining appears to have been adopted by the Vikings when they came into extensive contact with a money economy in Anglo-Saxon England, and the first Viking coins are those struck in the Viking colony of Dublin and by the Danes of the Danelaw in East Anglia.

All the Orcadian Viking hoards appear to be late. The Skaill hoard dates from the late tenth century, while another fairly large hoard from Burray dates from the early eleventh. This comprised 30 silver rings together with a silver armlet, a silver rod, an intertwined silver necklet, 108 pieces of silver cut off rings, a decorated ring and 3 silver coins of the Anglo-Saxon kings Edward the Elder, Edgar and Ethelred II. The hoard was contained in a wooden bowl. A small find from Stenness made in 1879 consisted of 4 gold rings, while a lost hoard also from the Stenness area consisted of 9 silver rings which were found in a mound near the Ring of Brodgar. A very large hoard, now unfortunately lost, was discovered at Caldale in 1774, not far from Kirkwall, and consisted of silver armlets and a horn containing 300 silver pennies of Cnut (1016–35).

The only comparable hoard from Shetland is one found in 1830 at Garthesbanks, Quendale, on Mainland. It comprised six or seven wristlets with a horn filled with Anglo-Saxon pennies of Ethelred II, Aethelstan, Edwy and Edgar. It is said that the hoard was found in the ruins of a building, with five broken vessels of steatite.

Viking houses

Early Norse at Jarlshof. Jarlshof is of paramount importance in any study of the Vikings in Scotland, since it remains the only settlement occupied for any length of time to have been extensively excavated (Fig 59; Pl 14).

When the Vikings arrived in the early ninth century, they found wheelhouse people still in occupation on the site. They chose for their farm a site on the landward side of the promontory, which they levelled prior to building a longhouse. This house, constructed of stones gathered from the beach, comprised two rooms, a kitchen and

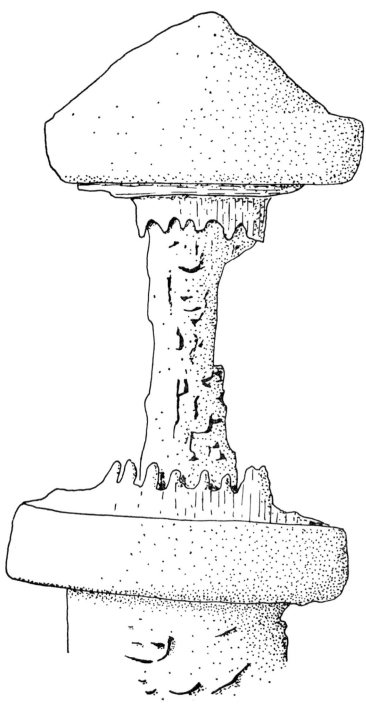

Fig 57   Viking sword hilt from a grave at Sweindrow, Rousay, Orkney

living room, with the main entrance leading into the kitchen through the north wall. The kitchen had in the centre of the floor a rectangular hearth with an adjoining oven or cooking pit, to enable red-hot stones to be tipped from the fire down the sloping slabs lining the cooking pit. In the living room a central hearth was again an important feature, and along the sides of the long walls were stone platforms or

Fig 58   The Maes Howe 'lion'

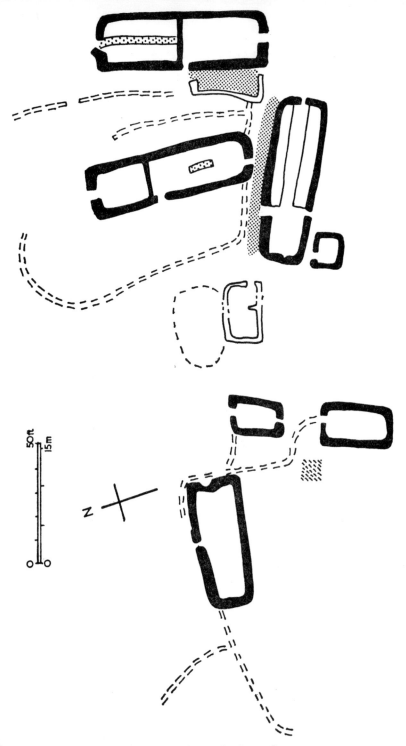

Fig 59 Jarlshof, plan of Norse settlement in the tenth century

benches on which tables and beds would have been set. The whole building had a timber roof, supported by timber posts in two rows along the edges of the platforms. The timber was quite possibly imported from Norway. A door in the east wall of the living room opened on to the slope behind the house, where there was a midden of burnt stones and peat ash. To the side of the house a circle of pebbles was found where a child had left them.

Beyond the kitchen lay the outbuildings—byre, smithy, barn and small outhouse—the last probably acting as servants' quarters. Nearby was another small building with a hearth, which may have been either a temple or a bath-house. The outbuildings were reached by a paved path from the kitchen door.

The servants were probably the native occupants of the now deserted wheelhouses and passage house, and objects of native late Iron Age type were found mixed with Norse in the midden. The type of house represented by this, the 'parent farmstead', at Jarlshof is not a true longhouse, in which dwelling quarters and byre are under one roof alignment, separated only by a cross-passage, but a variant form which was devised by the Norse in the Northern Isles. The true longhouse was however common in Scandinavia.

Farming appears to have been the main occupation of the first settlers. They kept sheep, pigs, cattle and ponies. In the early days of the settlement they do not appear to have engaged much in fishing, though a few line sinkers were found in excavation, and agriculture was not of great consequence either, though burnt grain and sickles were found belonging to this phase.

Slag was found in considerable amounts in the smithy. Here was also found a large pock-marked stone used as an anvil and a circular stone setting which had probably held a barrel of water for slaking the metal. Iron objects from the site included knife blades, hasps, sickles and strike-a-lights, as well as clinker nails for small boats.

Most of the small objects required in daily life were made on the site. Bone was fashioned into composite combs and pins, and antler was used for the same purpose. Some of the combs have interlace

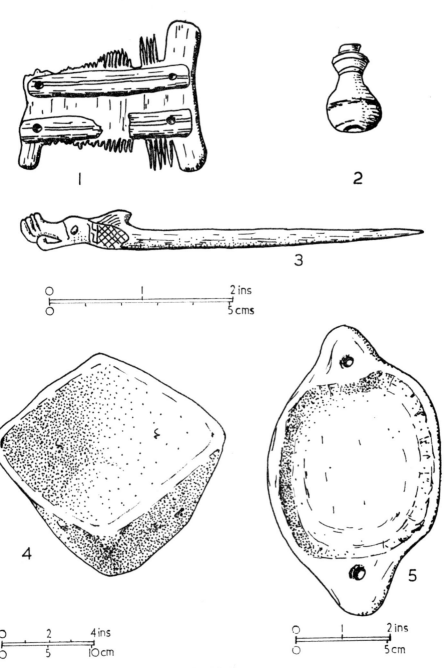

Fig 60   *Norse period objects from Jarlshof*
   1, 2, 3 Bone (approx actual size)
   4 Steatite (Scale: ¼)   5 Steatite (Scale: ½)

decoration engraved on them, while the pins include some with animal heads.

The early Norse did not use pottery, preferring instead vessels made out of steatite (soapstone), which is soft enough to be easily carved into pots. Initially such pots and other soapstone objects such as loom-weights were imported from Norway, and could easily have acted as ballast. Until the discovery of a local source of steatite 12 miles to the north at Cunningsburgh, broken fragments of steatite pots were used as loomweights, and when the supply of broken fragments ran out pebbles of schist and other stone were gathered from the beach for the same purpose. The steatite quarry at Cunningsburgh can still be seen. Here archaeologists found the sockets from which the blocks of stone for round-bottomed pots were quarried near the quarry face. Further up the hill were found the traces of the quarrying of soapstone for the type of square-sided pot popular at Jarlshof in the twelfth and thirteenth century, worked at a time when the more accessible supplies of the material had been exhausted.

An artist of some skill worked at Jarlshof early in the history of the settlement. A series of drawings executed on slate and sandstone were found, representing ships, animals and even portraits. The finest is a portrait of a young man with a beard and curly hair. The back of the same stone carries a depiction of an old man with a straggly beard and toothless gums. The artist may have had a pupil, for along with these fine sketches is an inept attempt to draw a hen (Fig 61). A further series depicts ships. One has a dragon prow, while another representation depicts mast, rigging, steering oar and oarsmen. Yet another shows a boat with a striped sail. On the reverse of the stone with the dragon prow there is a drawing of a cow with a knot in its tail.

Some of the Jarlshof Vikings may have engaged in piracy as a subsidiary activity. A Celtic mount from the site was probably raided from elsewhere in Scotland or Ireland, and converted into a brooch with the addition of a hasp and catch-plate. Down by the shore camp fires, probably of returning raiders, were found, with wood ash and fish bones. A bronze pin was associated with one. Other bronze pins from

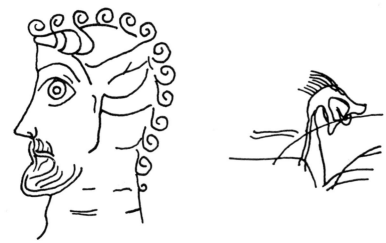

Fig 61   Norse drawings, Jarlshof

the site may also have been pillaged from other parts of Britain, though a series of ringed pins from Jarlshof are Norse copies of an Irish type. The only weapons found were an iron spear butt and spearhead, implying that the community was on the whole a peacefui one.

Jarlshof in the tenth century. The parent farmstead was extended in the mid-ninth century with the construction of a second farmhouse at right-angles to the first, running down the slope of the mound. This new farmstead, built possibly by the original farmer's son, has a stone-paved byre at the lower end, adjoining the kitchen. The temple or bath-house was allowed to fall into ruins, and was pulled down, being replaced by a stable range with cobbled floors. The yard was demarcated by a yard wall.

A third farmstead was built around 900, similar in general character to the second, which remained in use. As the area of settlement was now becoming crowded, the only subsidiary structure of the third farmhouse was an outhouse butted on to the building itself.

The development of a closely-knit community, as exemplified by

Jarlshof, seems to be characteristic of the Norse colonies in Scotland—
the same phenomenon can be seen at Birsay or at Freswick Links in
Caithness.

The tenth century witnessed the increasing importance of fishing
in the economy of the community, seal hunting being particularly
important. During this period a large midden of peat ash grew up on
the lower slope, eventually covering an area of over 5,000sq ft to a
depth of 3ft. Finds from this midden give a good impression of the
material possessions of the tenth-century Norse. Hemispherical
steatite pots were replaced by trough-shaped vessels, animal-headed
bone pins were replaced by simpler types with flat expanded tops, and
combs were plainer. Loomweights were now made exclusively out of
waterworn pebbles. Children's toys—tiny querns, line sinkers and
decorated bone pins for spinning on strands of wool—came from this
midden, as did small bone bits which, on analogy with later usage,
were put in lambs' mouths to prevent them sucking ewes' milk in late
spring.

The tenth-century Norse of Jarlshof had few impressive possessions,
to judge by the finds; but one fine gilt bronze strap-end decorated
with Ringerike-style ornament of the early eleventh century was found
at the top of the midden. At some stage in the tenth century the
occupants of Jarlshof became Christian, and cross-headed pins were
among the midden finds.

Underhoull. On Unst, the most northerly of the Shetland Islands, a
Norse house has been excavated within recent years which amplifies
the picture of life there. The house was boat-shaped, of the same type
as the first house at Jarlshof. It was constructed on the site of an earlier
Iron Age dwelling, and stone was robbed for its construction, a quern
being used as a kerbstone for the path. The construction technique
was standard for the Norse period in the Northern Isles—the walls
had stone facings on the inside and alternate stone and turf on the outside to render the building windproof. As the turf rotted the walls had
to be periodically rebuilt. A single line of posts supported the roof.

Drainage was difficult due to its position on the slope, and to solve this a good drainage system was constructed. It was a true longhouse, with a raised byre at the west end.

Occupation at Underhoull may have begun in the ninth century, but was particularly flourishing in the tenth. As at Jarlshof in this period, fishing played an important part in the economy, and finds included a stone vessel possibly for rendering down fish livers. A sandstone sharpening stone seems to have been used for honing fish hooks as well as pins and needles. A line sinker was also found. Steatite was used for making both rounded and squared bowls and for a baking board, and one fragment of a steatite bowl was associated with a slate chisel used in its manufacture. Spindle whorls, loomweights, lamps and toy millstones were among the other finds, while fragments of gaming boards and counters imply that board games were played here as at Jarlshof and Buckquoy in Orkney. Black pumice stone, found on the house floor, may have been used for finishing off wooden articles.

An associated boat noost (unroofed boat house) may also be Norse in date. It was built freestanding for a boat about 18ft long, and had a curved end some 4ft deep. A nearby midden, probably belonging to another house, produced an iron axe head and bones of cattle, sheep, pigs, rabbits and fish.

A corn drying chamber was added to the house at a late stage in its history, furnished with a central hearth round which ran a stone-lined channel, roofed in part with flat stones, which acted as a draught channel.

Norse houses in Orkney. A comparable series of Norse houses have been excavated in Orkney, of which the most notable are those on the Brough of Birsay, at nearby Buckquoy, at Westness on Rousay (where the building is in fact a hall), at Aikerness and at Skaill, Deerness.

At Buckquoy, on the mainland opposite the Brough of Birsay, three successive houses were excavated in 1970–1. The earliest, of uncertain date, had a byre at one end and measured about 24ft. It was subsequently used as a midden. The following house had a barn with a stone floor, while the latest, which had the tenth-century burial dug (see p 173) partly into it, had bowed walls and a paved yard. All were incomplete, and part of a larger complex—they had been in part eroded by the sea. Finds included the usual type of composite bone combs, small bone pins, spindle whorls and stone gaming boards, as at Jarlshof and Underhoull, used for a game like nine mens' morris.

The complex on the Brough of Birsay belongs to many periods down to the twelfth century and includes, apart from the Pictish remains, 'Earl Sigurd's Hall' and 'Earl Thorfinn's Palace' along with the cathedral complex. These buildings are all discussed in the next chapter (see p 191). Only the houses need be discussed here.

The houses belong mainly to two groups on the slope to the east of the cathedral complex. The earliest, known as Site C, comprise two houses side by side separated by a narrow paved passage. These are probably of ninth-century date and the oldest was altered in the tenth or eleventh century. On Site D nearby, three houses of the ninth, tenth and eleventh centuries were excavated; they were found to have been occupied successively. In general these houses are similar to those at Jarlshof, the earliest having stone facings to the inside of the walls and alternating stone and turf outside, the later ones having turf cores faced with stone both inside and out. The roofs were of turf, probably on wickerwork with a thatch covering.

Two rectangular stone settings less than 6ft square separated the northern house on Site C into two sections. These were probably the bases of wooden box beds which divided living room from byre. The living room had one corner paved for use as a smithy, and had a stone pillar set in the floor for an anvil.

The houses were probably accommodation for the officers and guard of the earl who lived on the brough, rather than farms, which are probably represented in the Buckquoy complex.

CHAPTER 7

Norse Golden Age and Later

NORSE BUILDINGS

From the establishment of the Norse earldom of Orkney around 880, until the thirteenth century Orkney was the centre of an important domain which stretched from Shetland to Caithness. The Earls of Orkney were virtually independent rulers, owing little but nominal allegiance to the kings of Norway or Scotland. The first earl was Sigurd the Mighty, who campaigned in Sutherland and Caithness, and was buried on the banks of the Oykell in the former county. Traditionally his nephew Einarr introduced the custom of peat cutting for fuel to the islands, and as a result acquired the epithet Torf.

About a century after Earl Sigurd's campaigns was born the second of the great Orkney earls, Thorfinn the Mighty, who was made earl of Caithness when he was only 5 years of age and who later became earl of both Orkney and Shetland. He was the grandson of Malcolm of Scotland, and following the death of Malcolm in 1033 he was forced to spend many years campaigning against a rival claimant to the earldom, Rognvald Brusason, who was finally slain in battle in 1046. The earlier part of Thorfinn's career was also taken up with campaigns against the Irish and against Duncan of Scotland; later he allied himself with Duncan's murderer, Macbeth, and acquired considerable estates on the Scottish mainland. Thorfinn appears to have felt guilty about the death of Rognvald, and travelled to Norway and then to Rome in order to obtain absolution from the Pope for his sins. On his return he built a cathedral at Birsay and lived on the tidal island until

his death. During his rule the Norse in the Northern Isles became formally Christian.

Thorfinn's grandsons were Haakon and Magnus. The latter was murdered by his brother on Egilsay, and was canonised as Saint Magnus, being buried on Birsay but later translated to the new cathedral in Kirkwall dedicated in his honour by his nephew Ragnald. Ragnald too was canonised, having led a crusade. He died in Caithness in 1158.

With Ragnald came to an end the great age of the Norse earldom. Norse earls still ruled until 1231, but from his death onwards there was increasing influence in the Northern Isles from the Scotto-Norman kingdom so that, in the twelfth century, the Scottish mainland was reclaimed from the Norse.

Brough of Birsay (Fig 63; Pl 11b)

The site of Brough of Birsay is perhaps the most symbolic of the Golden Age of the Norse earls.

The earliest building of the Norse period on the brough, apart from the houses described in the previous chapter, is a complex known as 'Earl Sigurd's Hall' which is partly incorporated in the later palace of Earl Thorfinn. The 'hall' was partly destroyed by the sea, but had turf-cored walls and appears to have been similar to the hall at Westness, which measured about 100ft long by 30ft wide, with internal divisions.

The building, together with middens of the tenth and eleventh centuries, is crowned by Earl Thorfinn's Palace, a complex building which may be of several phases of construction. It consisted of a large building on the north side of an enclosure which faced on to an open courtyard which lay to the south. This building was centred on a passage, rather more than a yard wide, which ran back from the centre of the south façade. It was carefully built with masonry similar to that used in the cathedral, set in clay or mortar, with carefully squared stones. The floors had flagstone pavements, the roof was of turf. To the east of the passage were located two rooms, one of which contained

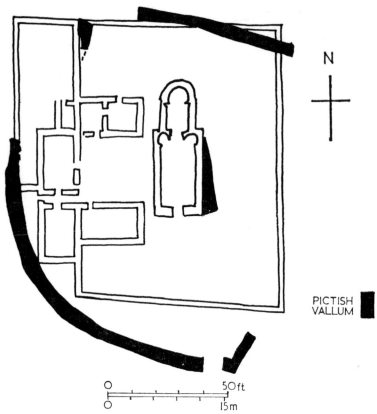

N

PICTISH
VALLUM

50 ft

15 m

Fig 63 Birsay—ecclesiastical site (after Cruden)

a firepit for the heating flues of the hall. The courtyard extended to the present cliff, where there was a bath-house. Apart from the main range, a western range consisted of two or three rooms running east and west, one of which had stone-faced earth benches on either side and a separate entrance to the main façade. Water was brought to an open basin between the benches through a stone-lined channel.

The palace in general is similar to the episcopal palace at Gardar in Greenland, though it is probably somewhat earlier and incorporates

192

some early features such as turf-cored walls. It is possible that the careful layout and good masonry was inspired by Thorfinn's visit to Rome.

The cathedral lay behind the palace complex. Although dedicated formally as Christchurch, it became known as St Peter's, and probably contained the relic of some saint that Thorfinn had brought back from Rome. The present remains are hardly suggestive of a cathedral, and indeed cathedral in this context only means principal minster, not necessarily a considerable edifice. The church comprises a nave, 29ft long by 16ft wide internally, a choir 11ft long and an apse 8ft deep. It was the original intention of the builders to construct a western tower, but this apparently was never completed. Structural evidence suggests that the church was built around 1050. In the north wall of the choir is a double splay window of a type found in Carolingian churches in the Rhineland and which in England would be considered Anglo-Saxon.

In the centre of the nave excavators found a grave containing a skeleton in a wooden coffin. The bones, which were disarticulated, had been put in the grave long after death. It has been supposed that this grave was that used originally for St Magnus and later after he was translated to Kirkwall re-used for some other notable, possibly the founder Earl Thorfinn himself. Round the church was a rectangular graveyard, with Norse burials laid in stone cists with cover slabs. Earlier cross slabs were used in a couple of cases as cover stones for later Norse burials.

Three ranges of buildings are grouped round a courtyard to the north of the church, the fourth range being taken up by the church itself. The north range was domestic, comprising a hall at the east end and a screen passage in the centre. The western room served as an antechamber, warmed by large fires, and the main entrance to the building was by way of this room, though this was later blocked. The west range, which is contemporary or slightly later, probably was a private apartment. The east range consisted in all probability of store-rooms, and was less well built. This curious complex appears to be contemporary with other modifications to the general plan of the site. The original entrance to the cemetery was blocked and a new entry made in the south wall of the enclosure. A new door was also cut in the north wall of the nave, and a paved passage led across the courtyard to a door at the end of the screens passage in the north range. About this time also two small side altars were set in circular recesses in the east corners of the nave. The closest parallels for them are from Trondheim and the cathedral at Gardar.

These important changes in the church and the construction of the subsidiary ranges of buildings are probably to be associated with the establishment of a bishopric at Birsay, sometime during the term of office of Bishop William, who died in 1168. The ranges of buildings probably constitute a twelfth-century bishop's palace, and the additional altars denote an increase in the number of resident clerics.

The last complex to be considered is the group of small houses overlying Earl Thorfinn's Palace. These consist of two or three small rooms each, and are quite unlike the earlier Norse houses, being more similar to medieval farmsteads. They are not however farmhouses, and are possibly the dwellings of the clergy who served the cathedral.

Twelfth-century churches

Orphir. Birsay is not the only church surviving from the Golden Age of the Norse earldom. The earliest, and indeed one of the most curious, is the ruined round church at Orphir. This stood until the eighteenth century, when it was partly demolished to make room for an extension to the parish church, which has itself been subsequently demolished. Originally it was 20ft in diameter with a stilted apse on the east. It stood 15ft high, and was lit by a circular opening in the vault and a small slit window in the apse. It is narrated in the *Orkneyinga Saga* that a 'noble church stood outside the hall door' at Orphir. The site of this Norse hall known as the Earl's Bu was partially excavated in the last century and some of the foundations are now visible outside the present churchyard wall. Mainly on the basis of the type of window, a date between 1090 and 1160 has been suggested for the building. It was known as the Girth House in recent times (from the Norse word for a sanctuary) and it seems probable that it was built by Earl Haakon Paulsson shortly after 1120, on his return from Jerusalem, where he had gone on a pilgrimage after the murder of St Magnus (Fig 64).

The round plan is probably modelled on the Church of the Holy Sepulchre at Jerusalem, but one need not see Earl Haakon's pilgrimage as the inspiration, for there are a series of such churches in northern Europe following this plan. One existed in the deserted medieval burgh of Old Roxburgh, but no trace survives; several others exist in England, though usually of larger dimensions, and frequently are associated with the Templars. The closest parallel for Orphir is the chapel at Ludlow Castle in Hereford, though this is a larger building.

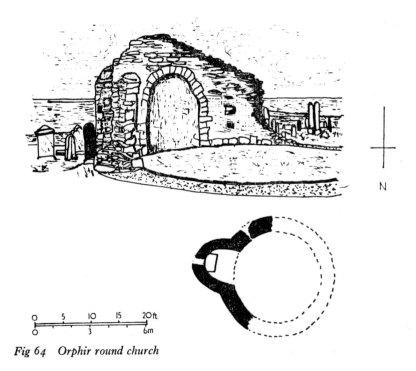

Fig 64   Orphir round church

In Europe, three chapels in Prague are even more similar. The plan seems to have become popular in Europe following the First Crusade.

St Magnus, Egilsay. A building in many ways closely related to Birsay is the church of St Magnus on Egilsay. It was on this island that the saint was murdered, and the church may possibly be connected with the event. Bishop William probably lived on Egilsay prior to his establishment of the bishopric at Birsay, and established the church around 1135, using it as his seat until the new church was built on the brough. It consists of a nave and chancel, opening directly on to the nave without a chancel arch. The chancel was surmounted by a barrel vault, now missing, above which was a chamber under the roof. Attached to the west end of the nave is a round tower, some 10ft in diameter. From the first stage of the tower a doorway gave access to the west end of the nave, and another door led from the chamber above the chancel vault, demonstrating that originally there were timber galleries and presumably staircases at first-floor level. The only entrance to the tower was through a door in the west wall of the nave. The doorways have round-headed 'Norman' arches. At the west end of the chancel the tusking of a stone screen is still traceable.

The most intriguing feature of Egilsay church is its similarity to Irish churches of the eleventh century. The round tower, for instance, is a feature fairly rare in medieval architecture. Apart from the series of later Anglo-Saxon examples in East Anglia, which are unlikely to have inspired Egilsay, there is another series in Ireland (with two surviving outliers at Brechin in Angus and Abernethy in Perthshire). Others may have existed in Scotland. Egilsay is the only surviving example attached to a church, but there was at least one other in Orkney. The parish church of Deerness for example, demolished in the eighteenth century, had two round towers flanking the west front, while the church at Stenness, also demolished in the eighteenth century, had a remarkable half-round tower at the west end. Both are known from eighteenth-century drawings, and Stenness was partly excavated in the earlier part of this century. There is reason to suppose that both

Deerness and Stenness were twelfth-century buildings. A twelfth-century hogbacked stone is still preserved in the vestry of the present church at Deerness (Fig 65).

The Irish round towers are for the most part detached from churches, as indeed were the two surviving Scottish examples. Originally built as belfries, as part of monastic complexes, they also served as watch towers and refuges for monks and their treasures at the time of the Viking raids. Access was far up the tower by means of a removable ladder; they had no staircases. It is probable that they were originally

Fig 65   Churches at Egilsay and Deerness from eighteenth-century drawings

attached to churches, later examples being free standing. The earliest surviving examples date from the tenth century, most are later, the best being mainly twelfth. About eighty survive in whole or in part.

Another Irish feature in St Magnus' is the chamber built above the vault. In Ireland such chambers arose when a relieving void was constructed beneath the stone roof, and were sometimes inhabited. The building as a whole is very similar to the church at Glendalough, County Wicklow, which dates from c 1100, where a round tower is attached to the west end, though here rising from a square annexe.

Eynhallow. A third large and unusual church survives from the twelfth century in Orkney. This is the building on Eynhallow ('holy island'). The island, now unoccupied, has a complex of buildings inhabited down to the nineteenth century and much altered in the sixteenth and seventeenth centuries. The only certain building is the church, which was converted into a two-floored dwelling probably in the sixteenth century, but restored shortly before it passed into the custody of the Department of the Environment in 1911. About 50ft externally, it consists of nave, chancel and west porch or tower, and has been extensively rebuilt. In the west gable of the porch or tower a door, 17in wide, is crowned with an arch consisting of two slanting slabs meeting at the top. The church probably dates from the twelfth century, and is related architecturally to those at Birsay and Egilsay.

In the complex to the west of the church is a chamber with projecting wing at the back and a passage along the front. The main block seems to have been two rooms, the passage being roofed with a pent roof butted on to the wall of the main block, which was probably two-storeyed. The date and character of this have been disputed, since little of the original masonry survives under later additions. It probably represents a twelfth-century monastic complex. That there was a monastery on Eynhallow seems fairly certain from the *Orkneyinga Saga*, which tells how a boy was kidnapped from the island in the mid-twelfth century. This boy, the son of Kolbein Hruga, was probably being taught by the monks there, and another reference tells how a refugee made his escape, by means of a boat belonging to monks, from an island which is almost certainly Eynhallow.

In the twelfth century it is unlikely that the claustral plan was in vogue in Orkney. The earliest claustral monastic complexes were only just being built at this time in the Scotto-Norman Lowlands, following the period of Anglo-Norman influence under the house of Canmore. In Ireland however plans similar to that at Eynhallow can be seen in some small Augustinian houses—Devenish, in County Fermanagh, is a good example; Kilmacduagh in County Clare is another.

Other churches. There are a few other churches of the period in Orkney, of less imposing character. The Cross Church on Westray, now roofless, has a nave and chancel and was originally barrel vaulted, the chancel being entered through a fine semi-circular arch. St Mary's Church, Pierowall, is another Westray church of the same general type, though it was probably built in the thirteenth century. It too has a nave and chancel, the latter out of line with the nave. In the seventeenth century it was much modified, the nave being widened and the chancel converted into a 'laird's aisle'.

St Mary's Church on Wyre, also has a nave and chancel, with a semi-circular arched doorway in the middle of the west gable of the nave and a semi-circular arch into the chancel. Originally the windows were round-headed. It was probably built in the late twelfth century by Kolbein Hruga, who built the castle nearby which bears his name (see p 201).

A number of smaller chapel sites in Orkney and Shetland conform to the same basic plan, and probably belong to the same period, such as the ruins of a church at Kirkaby, Westing, on Unst in Shetland.

Many of the twelfth-century churches were to become parish churches, but when built they were privately owned. The chapel selected for parish status was that built by the most important man in the parish.

St Magnus' Cathedral (Pl 16)

The most splendid building of medieval date in the Northern Isles is the cathedral of St Magnus in Kirkwall. It was, as already mentioned, founded by Rognvald, the nephew of St Magnus, who traditionally vowed in Norway to build a church in honour of his uncle. Work was commenced in 1137 under the supervision of Kol, Rognvald's father, and Rognvald himself. When funds ran low, Rognvald restored odal rights to the Orcadian farmers in return for a lump sum, which provided sufficient money for the work to continue. The cathedral shows close connections with Durham, and it seems almost certain that Durham masons had a hand in its construction. The fine red sandstone was brought from the Head of Holland, near Kirkwall. By the mid-thirteenth century the three bays of the choir, together with the transepts and an apse, appear to have been built. It is uncertain when it was consecrated, but it was used for sanctuary by 1154. By the early thirteenth century six bays of the nave were finished, closed by a temporary west gable. The original transeptal apses were demolished and replaced by chapels, and the crossing remodelled, possibly due to collapse. An extension of the choir, probably of French design and execution, followed in the second quarter of the thirteenth century. The tower on the crossing was added in the fourteenth century.

The Durham masons who worked on the cathedral probably came by way of David I's court on the Scottish mainland. Some architectural influences may have come from Norway, where there are certain similarities in the cathedral of Stavanger. The Romanesque work is extremely good, the later Gothic work slightly less accomplished.

Within the cathedral a number of burials have been found, including the remains almost certainly of Magnus and Rognvald, the former in a wooden coffin, set into piers probably in the sixteenth century. More interesting archaeologically is the grave of Bishop William, who died about 1168, and who was found reinterred beneath one of the north arches of the extended choir. This grave contained a staff head of bone and iron and a lead plate inscribed with a memorial formula. Another tomb of a bishop, supposedly that of Thomas Tulloch (c 1422–48) contained part of an oak crozier of indifferent workmanship and wax models of a chalice and paten. Another grave yielded a pewter or lead crozier and chalice and paten of the same metal. Such copies of more costly chalices and patens were usually buried in episcopal graves in the Middle Ages.

Norse castles (Fig 66).

The Norse were responsible for secular as well as ecclesiastical buildings in the Northern Isles. Most interesting among these is the castle of Kolbein Hruga on Wyre (known as Cubbie Roo's Castle).

Twelfth-century Norway was not feudal, and castles were rare. Not until the time of Haakon Haakonson (1217–63) were castles important in the country, though by the mid-thirteenth century Norse castle-building was in the mainstream of European developments. Although not building castles in their homeland in the twelfth century, the Norse must have seen such constructions in various parts of Europe, and imitated them in Scotland when the need arose. Norse Crusaders may have seen small towers in Provence when Sigurd and his followers went to the Holy Land in 1116. Earl Haakon may well have seen them on his journey to Rome in 1118, and Rognvald could well have seen them on his Crusade of 1152.

Cubbie Roo's Castle is a structure of many phases. The first is possibly the earthwork—a double bank and ditch—which may well be an Orcadian equivalent of the earthen ringworks of Norman defences. Such ringworks are known now from the Welsh Marches and also from southern Scotland, and appear to have been the forerunner of many later castles. They may even have pre-Norman origins in England.

The first stone-built phase consists of a small stone tower, a mere 15ft square internally, with walls 5ft thick, rising now to a height of about 6ft. There is no ground-floor entrance. It has two windows of slit formation, and in the centre of the floor a water tank is sunk into the living rock. Surrounding it are later additions. Excavation produced sherds of very coarse pottery of the type recently found at the Bishop's Castle, Scrabster, Caithness—a site also mentioned in the

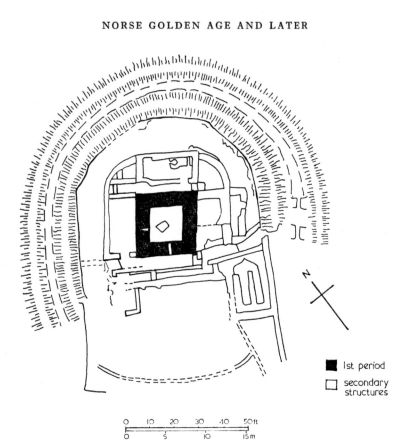

Fig 66   Cubbie Roo's Castle, Wyre

Orkneyinga Saga. Such pottery could quite easily be twelfth-century Norse.

The main reason for supposing that Cubbie Roo's is Kolbein Hruga's Castle lies in a reference in the *Orkneyinga Saga* which mentions his building a castle on Wyre. There is no other possible site on the island, and it is near St Mary's Church and the traditional site of his *bu* or drinking hall.

Another castle which may belong to this period is the Wirk, near the Viking site at Westness on Rousay. It has been much restored, probably in the sixteenth century. A number of other possible Norse castle sites are known, two, Castle Howe near the parish church at Holm and Cairnston near Stromness, still preserving some visible remains.

In the main these possible Norse castle sites are similar to some early castles elsewhere. The castle of Duniveg on Islay appears to be Norse, and even has what appear to be Norse longhouses in the enclosure. While much larger, the mainland castles of the twelfth to early thirteenth century seem to be basically keeps.

Jarlshof

Although the rich in the Northern Isles under the Norse earls built fine churches and possibly castles, life for the humbler farmers probably continued much as it had always done. The story is clearly told at Jarlshof, where the site continued to be occupied during the Golden Age.

During the eleventh century the secondary farmsteads seem to have been restricted in their expansion due to a shortage of land, and various attempts were made to obtain more accommodation. Within the yard walls stables or byres were built, but this still proved unsatisfactory and in due course all the secondary farmsteads were levelled to the foundations and new farmhouses were built over the foundations of the outhouses. The original farmstead remained in use, and the occupants appear to have converted the abandoned dwellings for their own uses.

The new houses at Jarlshof were smaller than the originals, built close together without yard walls between. This seems to accompany a change in the economy, which became predominantly fishing. Probably the settlement supplied fish to the southern part of Shetland Mainland. The 'parent farm' however remained devoted to farming, and continued to prosper. A byre was added at the east end. The kitchen also seems to have been enlarged, at the expense of the living quarters. In the twelfth century the parent house was finally abandoned, and the small fishing huts were enlarged into crofts with small byres. The parent farm was replaced by a new three-roomed dwelling, built at right-angles down the slope.

From the eleventh century onwards the site is less rich in material culture. The large round steatite bowls are replaced by square-sided vessels, quarried at Cunningsburgh. Bone objects are few, and consist mainly of pins and double-sided combs, the latter continuing until the late thirteenth century. Norse pottery appears for the first time, and consists of crude, steatitic pots mainly of jamjar shape. These were probably inspired by cooking pots imported from the east coast of the Scottish mainland, and sherds of such imported cooking pots were recovered in the late thirteenth- and early fourteenth-century levels. The remainder of the finds consist mainly of loomweights, line sinkers, steatite hanging lamps, hones, pot lids, spindle whorls and querns.

Towards the end of the thirteenth century the settlement declined. Many houses fell into disuse, and were replaced by a new farmstead which was not of Norse type, but which is included here to show the continuity of settlement on one particular site.

The medieval farmstead at Jarlshof (Fig 67). The medieval farmstead at Jarlshof appears to have been built towards the end of the thirteenth century. Although built in Norse style it is not of Norse type, nor does it conform to the usual medieval longhouse plan which may be inferred was current in mainland Scotland in the thirteenth and early fourteenth centuries. Its original layout consisted of two buildings, the largest being a rectangular dwelling house some 63ft by 20ft overall, with an annexe on its east side. The walls were built of stone with an earth core, continuing the Norse tradition. The house was originally entered through the annexe, and through doors in the west and south walls. The second building was a barn with a corn-drying kiln attached in the north-west corner. Pottery mixed with peat ash on the floor of the dwelling shows that its initial occupation was in the late thirteenth or early fourteenth century, and other finds include a bone playing piece and a bronze plaque reminiscent of heraldic horse pendants sometimes found on medieval sites.

The farmstead appears to have been occupied throughout the Middle Ages, with various modifications. Fourteenth- and fifteenth-century pottery was found on the site, continuing the farmhouse's story down to the final period of occupation of the site with the building of a sixteenth-century hall.

The corn-drying kiln in the farmhouse complex is remarkable for being circular rather than square. This form is typical also of Orkney,

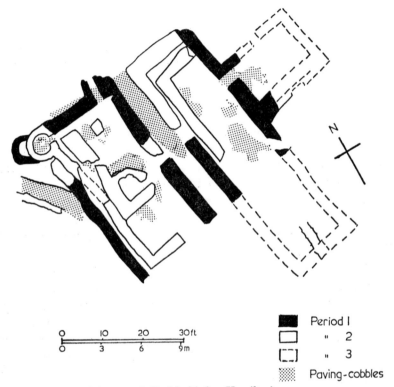

Period I
  "   2
  "   3
Paving-cobbles

Fig 67   Medieval farmstead, Jarlshof (after Hamilton)

whence it probably spread. The medieval farmstead should probably be seen as a hybrid between the old Norse longhouse type and the type probably introduced to the Northern Isles from the Scottish mainland in the thirteenth century. In spite of what has been written by Roussel and others there is little evidence for the survival of Norse building customs in the Northern Isles beyond this date.

Unfortunately, with the exception of Jarlshof, no other farmhouse of such medieval date exists from the Northern Isles.

Later Orkney farmsteads. Although Jarlshof's development ceased in the sixteenth century it is worth looking at the type of farmstead which ultimately evolved from such early structures. Most of the old Orkney farmsteads that survive date from the eighteenth or nineteenth century, though a few rare cases may possibly be from the sixteenth or seventeenth century.

The classic Orkney farmstead consists of an oblong block, single-storeyed, comprising the 'sellar' and the 'fire-house'. The sellar was an inner room, the fire-house the kitchen and living room. From each a further room projects. One of these smaller rooms was used as a store and was known as an 'ale-hurry', the other contained the box (or 'neuk') bed. Usually the byre was attached to this main range, while the subsidiary buildings, the stable, barn and corn kiln, adjoin. A number of recesses were built into the walls, some as cupboards, others as nesting boxes for geese. Two examples have curved backs: the 'sae bink' holding a water tub and the 'quern ledder' containing the grinding mill. In a few instances all the buildings may be under the same roof alignment. Masonry tends to be rough, depending on the quality of the building stone, and the roofs are thatched or covered with flagstone or turf. The fire was lit in the centre of the fire-house, usually against a stone pillar, the smoke escaping through the roof. A number of good examples can still be seen in Orkney, the best being Nether Benzieclett in Sandwick. The use of stone furnishings is reminiscent of Skara Brae.

An important element in the Orkney farmhouse, and to some extent in the Shetland farmhouse also, is the corn-drying kiln. Sometimes attached to the farmhouse, sometimes to a subsidiary building, it is a conical tower about 12ft in diameter and up to 15ft high, with a dished bottom into which the fire channel runs. The grain was laid on straw on a wooden framework, and hot air from the ingle hole at the bottom of the kiln passed along a vent upwards through the grain to a vent in the top of the kiln. Recently Mr Peter Gelling has excavated a six-teenth-century barn with corn-drying kiln at Skaill, Deerness, which architecturally is of the general type current at this later date in Orkney.

Two-storeyed buildings were rare in Orkney before the eighteenth century, and probably belonged to local lairds.

THIRTEENTH TO SIXTEENTH CENTURY

After the line of Norse earls came to an end in 1231, it was followed by Scottish earls, who owed allegiance to the Norwegian crown, though gradually Norse influence waned and finally came to an end politically in 1469. For the period from 1231 to 1469 documentary and archaeo-logical evidence is scanty and uninformative. In 1397 the Union of Kalmar had brought all Scandinavian countries under one monarch, and Denmark had retained the hegemony, so that by the mid-fifteenth century Norway had ceased to have an identity as a sovereign country. Thus Denmark regarded the Northern Isles as her possessions, the other remaining Scottish territories, the Western Isles, having already been lost in 1266 at the Treaty of Perth which followed the battle of Largs. In 1468 a marriage treaty was arranged between Denmark and Scotland, James III being promised to the daughter of Christian of Denmark in return for a considerable dowry. Christian was unable to raise the dowry, and the Northern Isles were pledged to cover it. Subsequent Danish attempts to redeem the pledge failed, and the islands were never restored.

The sixteenth century was a black period in the history of the Northern Isles, though archaeologically it produced a fine series of buildings. The earls responsible for the misery were the Stewarts. The first, Earl Robert, was the illegitimate son of James V, and built the Earl's Palace at Birsay. His son, Earl Patrick, was responsible for the building of the Earl's Palace at Kirkwall and the castle at Scallo-way in Shetland. He was executed with his son Robert in Edinburgh in 1615 on a charge of treason.

The castle builders (Figs 68–9)

A few sherds, most notably from Birsay, show that traders were bringing pottery from Yorkshire and eastern Scotland into the Northern Isles in the fourteenth century. What little ceramics exist from the later Middle Ages also appear to have been imported, though there may have been some local pottery industry in Shetland producing crude pots of Iron Age appearance. Documentary sources suggest that trade flourished—probably Bergen figured prominently as a trading partner with Kirkwall. Life in Orkney and Shetland must have continued on a fairly even tempo of fishing and farming, culturally sharing much in common with mainland Scotland.

Only one pre-Renaissance building of any consequence survives in the Northern Isles—the Bishop's Palace in Kirkwall (Pl 16). After the precocious period of castle construction in the twelfth century, the Northern Isles do not seem to have played any real part in the story of Scottish castle building. Although much altered the Bishop's Palace was basically an oblong building of red and white sandstone set alternately to give a polychrome effect: the same technique can be seen only in St Magnus' Cathedral. The palace dates from the early thirteenth century, and was presumably built for Bishop William when the bishop's seat was transferred to Kirkwall from Birsay. Architecturally, it has much in common with the castle of Bergen, and indeed King Haakon almost certainly died there in 1263. The original episcopal palace probably consisted of a hall-house, used for ceremonial occasions, and a tower house which formed the bishop's private residence. In plan this closely conforms to the royal palace at Bergen, with its festal hall built by Haakon IV and a tower house added by his son.

Alterations to the Bishop's Palace were made in the time of Bishop Reid (1541–58), when the building was in part demolished, then rebuilt, with the addition of the substantial round tower in the northwest corner. Later still, around 1600, Earl Patrick added buttresses and extensions.

The chief feature of Scottish castle building in the later Middle

Ages is the development of the tower house. While the last castles in England built solely for defence do not outlive the sixteenth century as residential sites, Scottish tower houses continued to be occupied during the seventeenth. Basically, a tower house is simply a medieval hall-house in which the domestic ranges are built upwards instead of on one level, for defensive purposes. Fourteenth-century tower houses, like Norman keeps in England before them, often had the entrance at first-floor level, approached by a ladder. The basic problem of maximum accommodation with maximum defence was answered in tower houses by a variety of solutions. Initially, extra accommodation was gained by means of appartments within the walls. Towards the end of the fourteenth century a wing was added for accommodation, known as a 'jam', resulting in an L-shaped plan. This had the added advantage of giving protection for the main door in the re-entrant angle, which could be covered by both the main tower and the wing. Towards the end of the fifteenth century the widespread use of arms necessitated further developments, and the Z-plan was developed—a major feature of sixteenth-century architecture. In such castles a wing is set out diagonally at each corner with gun loops to command the sides of the building. This allowed the wings or towers to give cover to the walls, and the main building in turn to cover the towers. The diagonal setting of the towers had the added advantage of not obscuring the light from the main block. About sixty examples of Z-plan castles are known, most of them in the north-east.

Both Muness and Scalloway castles in Shetland and Noltland in Orkney are good examples of Z-plan architecture. Muness Castle on Unst is the most northerly castle in the British Isles, and is a gaunt and depressing edifice, built in 1598. Scalloway Castle (Pl 15a) was built in 1600, by Earl Patrick, and traditionally blood was mixed with mortar in its construction—a legend which occurs in the story of several castles and which may be derived from fact. Scalloway is really an example of the type of plan intermediate between L-plan and Z-plan, in which the wing or jam is set diagonally to the corner of the building. It is particularly well preserved. Noltland Castle on Westray

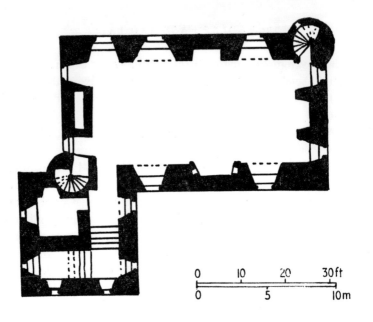

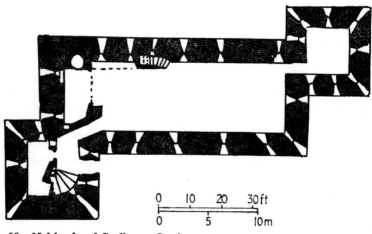

Fig 68   Noltland and Scalloway Castles

is of Z-plan, and was built between 1560 and 1573 by Gilbert Balfour. Its most notable feature is its complex arrangement of tiers of gun loops.

Other examples of sixteenth-century castle architecture are the Earl's Palace at Birsay, to the east of the Brough of Birsay complex, and the Earl's Palace at Kirkwall. The former is now much ruined, and is in the process of consolidation, during which it is hoped the plan will be clarified. It was built for Earl Robert in 1574, with narrow ranges grouped about an open court. Initially these probably occupied two sides, the range opposite the entrance being a hall with solar and kitchen. The fourth side may have been merely a curtain wall, but this was extended into a domestic range. Recent clearance has revealed a fine tiled floor of intricate pattern. Although now stark, the facing would have been harled over with a type of rough-cast in grey/white; keying for the harling is still visible on the outer stonework. The Earl's Palace in Kirkwall however remains as the most outstanding example of Stewart architecture. It is one of the finest examples of Renaissance architecture in Scotland and, apart from its roof, is almost complete.

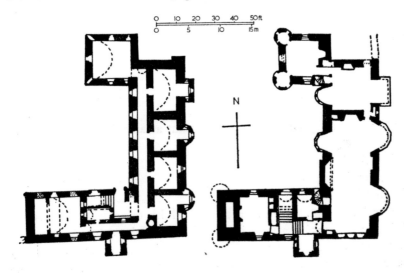

Fig 69   Earl's Palace, Kirkwall

Like the palace at Birsay it is grouped round a square court, though it only occupies three sides. It was built by Earl Patrick between 1600 and 1607, and never completed. In concept it is akin to Elizabethan architecture in England, and its most striking feature is its use of oriel windows, corbelled out, in the French manner (Fig 69).

These northern castles seem closely related. The Earl's Palace at Kirkwall, the castles of Scalloway, Muness and part if not all of Noltland were the work of the same architect. Apart from similar details, such as the form of their gun loops, they all show the same competence in the handling of staircases. Noltland has a spiral staircase of the traditional type, though wider and grander than those usually found in contemporary Scottish castles. The others however have stairs in flights and landings, integrated with the rest of the plan, and show considerable awareness of spacial effect, varying ceiling heights and vaults to give particularly satisfying vistas.

Other sixteenth and seventeenth century buildings in the Northern Isles are much less remarkable and well preserved. In view of its recent restoration and conversion into a museum, mention however should perhaps be made of Tankerness House in Kirkwall (Pl 15b). Approached from the street by an arch surmounted by a small balcony with an armorial panel, the ranges are grouped about an open court of picturesque character. Built at different times, the whole is the product of the sixteenth century, and behind it lies a fine garden. Restored, it suggests admirably that life, at least for the rich, in sixteenth-century Orkney was as pleasant as anywhere in Scotland.

'Click' Mills—an epilogue (Fig 70)

The antiquities of the eighteenth and nineteenth centuries are more the province of the architectural historian or student of folk life than the archaeologist. For the architectural historian, the Hanoverian defences of Fort Charlotte in Lerwick, related as they are to Fort George at Inverness or Fort Augustus, are important and historically interesting remains of a stirring period in Scotland's past. The importance of the Northern Isles as a base for maritime operations has long

Fig 70   Dounby 'Click' Mill

been recognised—Charles II built a fort at Lerwick, while Cromwell built a fort at Kirkwall. The Churchill Barriers, with their attendant wrecks, not to mention the Italian Chapel on Lamb Holm and the nearby pillboxes will no doubt in time become the source material for future archaeologists and historians concerned with World War II.

One category of recent monument is perhaps worthy of a place at the end of this survey. This phenomenon, the horizontal mill, is a familiar feature of Shetland, and to a lesser extent Orkney. Believed to be a Norse introduction (though this is debatable) these tiny mills have horizontal instead of vertical wheels, and derive their name from the noise they make as the water flows under them from the lade. They are simply a development of the old hand quern, operated by what is in effect a water turbine. That at Troswick Mill at Dunrossness in Shetland still grinds poor-grade barley and oats, while another, restored by the Orkney Society in 1932 and now in the guardianship of the Department of the Environment, is a fine tourist attraction at Dounby. Although it grinds no grain, the machinery is still intact, and the sound it makes is a pleasant echo from the past.

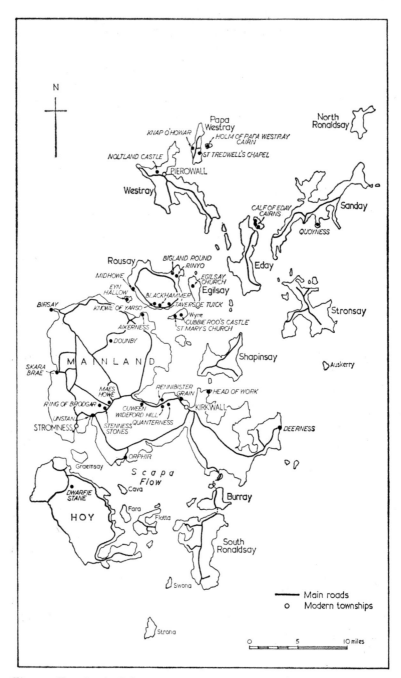

Fig 71   Key sites in Orkney

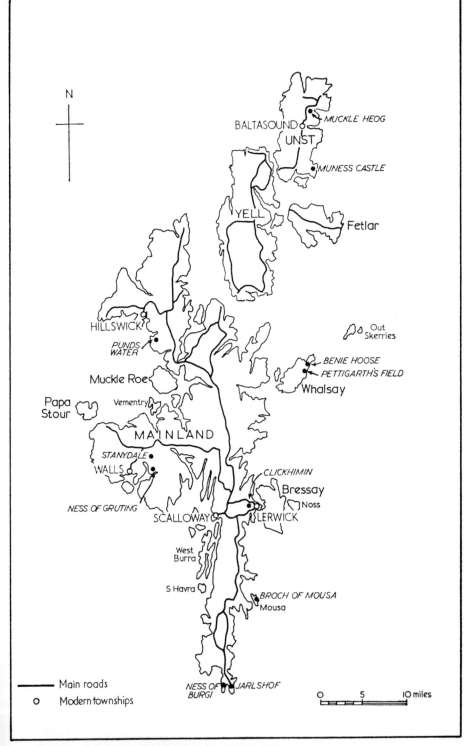

Fig 72 Key sites in Shetland

Glossary

Artefact   A man-made object

Ashlar   Dressed masonry of squared blocks of stone

Barrow   A mound heaped up over a burial deposit. The term is normally used of mounds of earth, *see also* Cairn

Berm   The space left between a ditch and the bank of upcast earth. This level space prevents the upcast sliding back into the ditch due to weather erosion, and can also act as an additional defence

Cairn   A mound composed of stones or lumps of rock, normally covering a funerary deposit. Cairns can, in some instances, be simply mounds of stone erected as landmarks on hills or other prominent positions, or be clearance stone-heaps from fields. In archaeological literature however the term 'cairn', without further qualification, can be taken to mean a burial mound

Complex   A complex is an assemblage, normally of buildings or other structural features, which taken together seem to have a meaningful relationship. Less frequently the term is used to denote a group of artefacts which appear to be related but do not necessarily amount to a culture

Corbelling   In prehistoric and early medieval archaeology this means that a primitive dome is constructed by oversailing (projecting) each course of walling with the next, until the walls converge. A corbel in medieval architecture is a projecting stone in a wall intended to take a timber beam or an overhanging wall

Culture   Where certain types of artefacts and structures occur associated within a limited area, and it can be demonstrated that they do not similarly occur associated in other areas, the assemblage is termed a culture. Essentially, a culture must constitute the archaeological evidence for a group of people or a society in anthropological terms. A group of objects is not normally sufficient evidence for the recognition of a culture, unless the objects are of sufficiently varied types—house types, funerary custom and religious monuments should also be taken into consideration

Deposit A deposit is a group of artefacts buried at the same period, normally in the same archaeological stratum

Drystone masonry Masonry constructed without the use of mortar

Herringbone masonry The technique of building with thin slabs set at an angle in alternate courses

Industry A recurring assemblage of a particular type or types of tools. The term is normally used in studying the Stone Age where flint tools are the only available artefacts, and which in themselves are not sufficient for the recognition of a culture

Megalith Strictly speaking, a very large stone. The term is normally used of Neolithic chambered tombs which employ undressed stones of exceptional size

Orthostat A standing stone; the upright as opposed to the capstone in a megalithic structure

Penannular Almost a ring. The term is often used of circular structures, particularly earthworks, with one entrance, and is also applied to a class of brooch which has a break for the pin

Post-hole Where a timber post has stood in a socket in the ground it will, after it has been removed or destroyed, leave a hole filled with earth of a different nature from the surrounding soil. This is termed a post-hole

Quern A stone hand-mill for grinding grain

Runes A type of alphabet using twig-like signs, employed by the Vikings

Scarcement A ledge of masonry set back in a wall, sometimes used to carry timbers of a floor or lean-to structure

Skeuomorph   Something which was once functional but has ceased to be so and which is retained for decorative effect

Spindle whorl   A small weight put on the bottom of a spindle to enable it to rotate more readily

Stratigraphy   In archaeological excavations it is normally the case that layers have been laid down which appear as different types of soil; excavation involves stripping these off one at a time and recording what they contain. The study of this is termed stratigraphy, and the relationship of finds to layers is known as the stratigraphical relationship. Normally the latest objects and structures are stratified above the earliest

Tumulus   A mound, either of earth or stone, covering a burial deposit

Tusking   Projecting stones from a wall, usually left when a wall has been demolished and the bonding stones are left in

Unicameral   Having only one chamber

Vallum   A bank of earth which defines the area of an ecclesiastical enclosure in the early Christian period. This may be a cemetery or a monastery

Further Reading

GENERAL

The standard work on the archaeology of Orkney and Shetland is F. T. Wainwright *The Northern Isles* (1962), which contains a very extensive bibliography. The serious student will also find essential the Royal Commission on Ancient Monuments (Scotland)'s *Inventory of Orkney and Shetland*, 3 vols (1946), now unfortunately out of print.

For background reading on Scottish archaeology, the most recent authoritative account is to be found in S. Piggott (ed), *Prehistoric Peoples of Scotland* (1962), the standard account, now alas very out-of-date, being V. G. Childe, *The Prehistory of Scotland* (1934). Two other short studies will be found invaluable for the less archaeologically minded: S. Piggott and W. D. Simpson, *Scotland* (1970), being the 6th edition of the series of illustrated guides to the ancient monuments in the care of the Dept of the Environment (this is the 6th volume in the series); and S. Piggott and K. Henderson, *Scotland before History* (1958). The former, apart from its excellent introductory text, has a list of all the ancient monuments in Scotland under state protection; the latter is an extended essay with unusual and evocative illustrations. Two other general books on Scottish prehistory may also be mentioned, both by R. Feachem: *Prehistoric Scotland* (1963) which is a gazetteer, and *The North Britons* (1966) which is a more general introductory to the archaeology of Northern Britain as a whole.

Those seeking a general introduction to the Islands as a whole (not merely from an archaeological standpoint) should consult the volumes on *Orkney* and *Shetland* in the David & Charles series on islands.

NEOLITHIC

The standard work on Scottish chambered tombs is A. S. Henshall, *The Chambered Tombs of Scotland*, 2 vols (1965 and 1972). The chambered tombs of the Northern Isles are discussed in vol 1, but vol 2 should also be consulted since it discusses the problems of chambered tombs as a whole in Scotland, and raises certain topics relating to the Northern Isles not mentioned in vol 1. Detailed bibliographical references to individual sites are also given.

Among the books and articles published since *The Northern Isles* and relevant to this area, the following may be cited as noteworthy: I. McInnes, 'A Scottish Neolithic Pottery Sequence', *Scottish Archaeological Forum*, 1 (1969), 19–30; A. S. Henshall, 'The Long Cairns of Eastern Scotland', *Scottish Archaeological Forum*, 2 (1970), 29–45; T. G. E. Powell (ed), *Megalithic Enquiries in the West of Britain* (1969) for recent theories on the origins of chambered tombs; G. Wainwright and I. Longworth, *Durrington Walls* (1970), Society of Antiquaries of London Research Report 29, for grooved ware and current thoughts on 'Rinyo-Clacton'; C. T. S. Calder, 'Cairns, Neolithic Houses and Burnt Mounds in Shetland', *Proc Soc Ant Scot*, 96 (1962–3), 37–86; C. S. T. Calder, 'Excavations in Whalsay, Shetland, 1954–5', *Proc Soc Ant Scot*, 94 (1960–1), 28–45.

BRONZE AGE

Very little has been published on the Bronze Age in the Northern Isles. An important work has been published however on the Beaker period generally, which affects the Northern Isles—D. Clark, *Beakers of Great Britain and Ireland* (1970). The metalwork of the Scottish Bronze Age has been discussed in detail in three articles by J. M. Coles: 'Scottish Early Bronze Age Metalwork', *Proc Soc Ant Scot*, 101 (1968–9), 1–110; 'Scottish Middle Bronze Age Metalwork', *Proc Soc Ant Scot*, 97 (1963–4), 82–156; 'Scottish Late Bronze Age Metalwork', *Proc Soc Ant Scot*, 93 (1959–60), 16–134. Of these, the last is the most important, since its implications extend to the Northern Isles.

IRON AGE

The early Iron Age has been the subject of considerable research in recent years. J. R. C. Hamilton's *Excavations at Clickhimin, Shetland* (1968) advanced one view of broch origins. Another viewpoint has been advanced in a series of papers by Euan MacKie: 'Brochs and the Hebridean Iron Age', *Antiquity*, 39 (1965), 266–78; 'The Origin and Development of the Broch and Wheelhouse Building Cultures of the Scottish Iron Age', *Proc Prehist Soc*, 31 (1965), 93–146; 'Radiocarbon Dates and the Scottish Iron Age', *Antiquity*, 43 (1969), 15–26; 'The Scottish "Iron Age"', *Scottish Hist Rev*, 49 (1970), 1–32; 'Some Aspects of the Transition from the Bronze to Iron-Using Periods in Scotland', *Scottish Arch Forum*, 3 (1970), 55–72; 'English Migrants and Scottish Brochs', *Glasgow Arch Journal*, 2 (1971), 39–71. Two other studies opposing MacKie have been published by D. V. Clarke: 'Small Finds in the Atlantic Province: Problems of Approach', *Scottish Arch Forum*, 3 (1971), 22–54; 'Bone Dice and the Scottish Iron Age', *Proc Prehist Soc*, 26 (1970), 214–32. Apart from these specific studies, A. L. F. Rivet (ed), *The Iron Age in North Britain* (1966), deals with problems in the Northern Isles among other topics.

EARLY CHRISTIAN PERIOD

The ecclesiastical archaeology of the Northern Isles is dealt with in passing in A. C. Thomas, *The Early Christian Archaeology of North Britain* (1969). Pictish art is discussed in three recent papers: A. C. Thomas, 'Animal Art of the Scottish Iron Age', *Arch Journal*, 118 (1961), 14–64; A. C. Thomas, 'The Interpretation of the Pictish Symbols', *Arch Journal*, 120 (1963), 31–97; I. Henderson, 'The Meaning of the Pictish Symbols', *The Dark Ages in the Highlands* (1971), 53–67. The subject is also dealt with in I. Henderson, *The Picts* (1964).

St Ninian's Isle treasure has resulted in numerous publications. The definitive report has been published in 1973 as A. Small (ed), *St Ninian's Isle and Its Treasure*, and reference should also be made to D. M. Wilson, 'Reflections on the St Ninian's Isle Treasure', *Jarrow*

Lecture, 1969; A. C. O'Dell *et al*, 'The St Ninian's Isle Silver Hoard', *Antiquity*, 33 (1959), 241–68; K. Jackson, 'The St Ninian's Isle Inscription: A Re-appraisal', *Antiquity*, 34 (1960).

A survey of Shetland early Christian sites has appeared as A. D. S. Macdonald and L. R. Laing, 'Early Ecclesiastical Sites in Scotland: A Field Survey, Part I', *Proc Soc Ant Scot*, 100 (1967–8), 123–34. Orkney Pictish stones are listed in J. N. G. Ritchie, 'Two New Pictish Symbol Stones from Orkney', *Proc Soc Ant Scot*, 101 (1968–9), 130–3.

The period generally is discussed in L. R. Laing, *The Archaeology of Late Celtic Britain and Ireland* (1974).

VIKING AND LATER MEDIEVAL

Very little has been published on this period since *The Northern Isles*. The excavations at Underhoull have been published as A. Small, 'Excavations at Underhoull, Unst, Shetland', *Proc Soc Ant Scot*, 98 (1964–6), 225–48. General study of the area is provided in A. Small, 'The Viking Highlands, A Geographical View', *The Dark Ages in the Highlands* (1971), 69–90. Placenames are covered in W. E. H. Nicolaisen, 'Norse Settlement in the Northern and Western Isles', *Scot Hist Rev*, 48 (1969), 6–17. Pierowall is re-assessed in A. Thorsteinnson, 'The Viking Burial Place at Pierowall, Westray, Orkney', and in A. Nicolaisen (ed), *Fifth Viking Congress* (1968), 150–73. Viking burial at Aikerness is described in W. N. Robertson, 'A Viking Grave found at the Broch of Gurness, Aikerness, Orkney', *Proc Soc Ant Scot*, 101 (1968–9), 289. The period is also discussed in general in L. R. Laing, *The Archaeology of Late Celtic Britain and Ireland* (1974).

Gazetteer

The Gazetteer lists alphabetically sites in the Northern Isles which are particularly worth visiting. To some extent the choice is arbitrary, for although some sites such as Jarlshof, Clickhimin or Skara Brae would appear in any such list, others are to some extent a matter of personal choice. In making this selection an endeavour has been made to list typical sites of all periods—few would consider, for example, that Fan Knowe Burnt Mound was of comparable interest to Maes Howe for the visitor, yet it is typical of similar extremely common burnt mounds in Orkney. Accessibility has been considered of major importance in compiling the selection, and preference has always been shown for a typical monument located near a major site rather than for a perhaps better preserved site that might require a considerable time and effort to reach. A few sites have been included because excavation has proved them to be of exceptional importance; for example the site of the Neolithic village of Rinyo has been included, although there are almost no surface indications of its existence.

The sites are listed alphabetically for each island, and the National Grid Reference is given to enable them to be located on the Ordnance Survey 1in sheet for the area. This is followed by a brief location description giving the road number where this is applicable and the best direction to approach the site.

Many of the main Orkney monuments are in the care of the Department of the Environment, fewer in the case of Shetland. Where such monuments are indicated in the Gazetteer public access is available and in summer they are signposted—visitors at Easter may find the signs have been taken down for repainting! The other sites are on private land, and permission to visit them should always be sought from the landowner or tenant.

The Northern Isles can be approached by air from Edinburgh, Glasgow, Aberdeen, Inverness or Wick (there are linking flights) or by sea. For those not in a hurry, perhaps the best approach is overland to Scrabster (the port of Thurso in Caithness) and thence by ferry to Stromness in Orkney, past the Old Man of Hoy. This ferry takes cars. Another ferry links John o' Groats with the island of South Ronaldsay, from which one can travel overland by way of the Churchill Barriers to the Orkney Mainland. This ferry does not take cars. Shetland can be reached by air from Orkney. For travel on the Orkney or Shetland Mainland a car is an advantage, as public transport is confined to the main routes and sites are often far from these. An inter-island air service operates in Orkney, visiting the main islands. Archaeologically minded visitors however are warned that the flight only operates (1972) once a day. In order to have time to visit monuments it is therefore usually necessary to stop overnight, for which arrangement in advance is advisable. An inter-island boat service also operates from Kirkwall.

Hotels exist on the Orkney and Shetland Mainland, notably in Kirkwall, Stromness, Lerwick and Scalloway; there are hotels on a few of the other larger islands, notably Westray and Sanday in Orkney and Yell and Unst in Shetland, but accommodation on the small islands (where it exists) is usually at private houses or farms.

Apart from site museums at Skara Brae, Birsay and Aikerness in Orkney and at Jarlshof in Shetland, there are good collections illustrating local archaeology at Tankerness House in Kirkwall and in Lerwick.

Finally, intending visitors are reminded that the Northern Isles have much else apart from archaeological remains, being of particular interest to the naturalist and fisherman. A picnic basket is always a useful asset, as suitable places for refreshment are few and far between, even on the Orkney and Shetland Mainland.

ORKNEY

The only site on Mainland that is difficult of access is the Brough of Birsay, which is on a tidal island approached across a causeway at low tide. It is however possible to cross at all times except the three hours on either side of high tide. Rousay can be reached by a regular ferry service. The same boat sometimes visits Egilsay, Eynhallow and Wyre, and it may be possible to go with it; at other times it is usually possible to hire transport for a visit. Hoy is reached by ferry from Stromness. Most of the other islands can be reached by the regular boat service, with the exception of Holm of Papa Westray and Calf of Eday for which special boat hire is necessary.

MAINLAND

1 *Aikerness, the Broch of Gurness*
NGR HY 383268
Location: About 11 miles NW of Kirkwall, along the A966 to Evie. The site lies on the coast looking out towards Rousay, about 1½ miles from the main road. The final approach is by foot.
Description: This Iron Age site was partially excavated in the 1930s and is now in the guardianship of the Department of the Environment. It consists of a broch, still preserved to a height of about 10ft, defended by a rock-cut ditch defence. In the post-broch period there was secondary occupation within the broch itself, and a settlement of huts grew up round it. Finally, there is a Viking burial and Norse settlement on the site.

2 *Bimbister*
NGR HY 329163
Location: A986 from Birsay to Boardhouse, and side road. The site is visible from the road.
Description: A typical example of an old Orkney farmhouse, with the corn-drying oven at one end. The Bimbister house is probably fairly recent (nineteenth century), but there are others in Orkney, like Nether Benzieclett, which may date from the sixteenth or seventeenth century. Dwelling and byre are under the same roof alignment.

3   Birsay—the Earl's Palace
NGR HY 246280

Location: 1 mile E of the Brough, near the shore, at the end of the A966.

Description: This palace was built for Robert, Earl of Orkney, in 1574. It is in the process of consolidation (1972), and is not well preserved. The building is on a courtyard plan, with rectangular towers projecting at three corners. It poses many architectural problems. An interesting feature is a tile mosaic floor. It is in the guardianship of the Department of the Environment.

4   The Brough of Birsay
NGR HY 239285

Location: On the north side of Mainland, 20 miles NW of Kirkwall. The site is on a tidal island, approached by a causeway.

Description: The earliest occupation on the site is Pictish, and the Pictish cemetery was excavated below the later Norse, producing a sculptured stone apparently associated with a burial. A facsimile of the stone stands on the site. Also Pictish was a metalworking site. In the Norse period 'Early Sigurd's Hall' was built on the edge of the cliff and this and the later Earl Thorfinn's Palace can still be seen, as well as the remains of Norse houses. The most substantial remains however are of the ruined twelfth-century church and associated structures. It is in the guardianship of the Department of the Environment.

5   Cuween Hill
NGR HY 364128

Location: On the side of Wideford Hill, not far from the Wideford Hill cairn. It is approached by the A965 from Kirkwall, and is about ½ mile S of Finstown, 6 miles WNW of Kirkwall. Access involves a climb across the slopes of Wideford Hill.

Description: A good example of a Maes Howe type of tomb, about 55ft in diameter and 8ft 6in in height. It has no external features and is grassed over. An 18ft passage leads down to the main chamber, the first 8ft 3in taking the form of a trough outside the tomb, the remainder incorporated in the mound. The main chamber is roughly rectangular, and stands to a height of over 7ft. From the main chamber four subsidiary compartments open out. When opened, the remains of men, dogs and oxen were encountered. In Department of Environment guardianship.

6 Deerness
NGR HY 088596
Location: On the east of the island, by the A960 and B9050 from Kirkwall. The site should be approached from Skaill. A footpath leads along the cliff (where there is an army range) past the impressive Gloup. The Brough of Deerness on which the site stands can be approached by the intrepid with a rock climb, the old land bridge is not now negotiable.
Description: A classic example of an early Christian monastic community, now much disturbed as a result of being used for target practice. The remains comprise a small rectangular oratory and a series of rectangular cells on a headland cut off by a stone-built vallum.

7 Dounby
NGR HY 325228
Location: On the B9057, about 2 miles NW of Dounby, approached across the fields.
Description: A good example of a horizontal mill of a type once widespread in the Northern Isles, the waterwheel being horizontal instead of vertical. This small example, now in the guardianship of the Department of the Environment, is notable in that it still works, but the key to turn on the water is not always available. The building is fairly modern (nineteenth century). Such mills are often called 'click mills' on account of the noise they make.

8 Fan Knowe
NGR HY 300198
Location: Adjoining the A986, about ¾ mile SE of Dounby.

Description: A good example of a type of monument common in both Orkney and Shetland. Although dating evidence is not available for the Northern Isles, evidence from Ireland suggests that they mark communal cooking places used in later prehistoric and early Christian times. The mounds are composed of heat-cracked stones, sometimes associated with food refuse. A few have associated stone cists, into which the heated stones were thrown to boil water.

9   *Five Hillocks*
NGR HY 460054
Location: In exposed terrain, approached by the A961 going south from Kirkwall. The site is about ¼ mile from the main road, near Rasheyburn.
Description: Six barrows, presumably of Bronze Age date, ranging from 12 to 20yd in diameter. All but one show signs of having been dug into, though no record of excavation survives.

10   *Grain*
NGR HY 442117
Location: About ¾ mile NW of Kirkwall, along the A965. The site is in Hatston airfield, no longer used for planes but continuing in use as an improvised housing estate. Its position is not easy to locate due to all the roads and buildings looking alike, but it is normally signposted.
Description: One of two Orcadian souterrains in the guardianship of the Department of the Environment. A flight of steps (some modern) lead down to a subterranean passage which terminates in a chamber with a slab roof supported on pillars. Among many inscriptions in the chamber should be noted an early one of Hugh Marwick, possibly the youthful scribing of the well-known local antiquary.

11   *Head of Work*
NGR HY 483138
Location: NE of Kirkwall, about 2½ miles along a side road to Work, thereafter on foot to the headland.
Description: This monument now appears as a grassy ridge, 153ft long

and averaging about 40ft wide. The east end of the cairn is higher than the west and has been disturbed; stones projecting from the turf indicate a chamber. At each end there are 'horns' projecting to form a forecourt. The tomb is most likely an Orkney-Cromarty type of chambered tomb, but is distinguished by being probably multi-period.

12 *Kirkwall—Bishop's Palace*
NGR HY 447108
Location: In the middle of Kirkwall, just south of the cathedral.
Description: This very ruined structure, now in the guardianship of the Department of the Environment, is structurally complex. The earliest phase may have been a twelfth-century hall-house, the masonry of which was later incorporated in additional work. The two main later building phases are those of Bishop Reid (1541–8) who added a round tower, and Patrick Stewart, Earl of Orkney, who completed the building c 1600.

13 *Kirkwall—the Earl's Palace*
NGR HY 448108
Location: Immediately to the south of the Bishop's Palace.
Description: One of the finest examples of Renaissance architecture in Scotland, though now ruined. It was built round three sides of a square by Earl Patrick Stewart between 1600 and 1607, but was not completed. Notable features are oriel windows, which are corbelled out from the wall, and an ornate fireplace.

14 *Kirkwall—Tankerness House*
NGR HY 447107
Location: Near the cathedral in the centre of Kirkwall.
Description: An extremely good example of a sixteenth-century town house, now restored as a museum by Kirkwall Town Council. In layout it is grouped about a picturesque courtyard, approached from Broad Street by an arched close surmounted by an armorial panel. It was owned by the Baikies, an old Orkney family.

15 The Knowe of Smirrus

NGR HY 291215

Location: ½ mile N of Dounby, off the A986. It is about ¼ mile from the main road.

Description: A Bronze Age cairn, notable for its size. It measures nearly 100ft in diameter, and stands to a height of about 6ft. It has been badly disturbed, which gives it an oval appearance, with a hollow in the centre. A disturbed cist or chamber can be seen in the centre.

16 Knowes of Trotty

NGR HY 341175

Location: A986 and B road. A farm road signposted to Millhouse should be followed; the Knowes are visible from immediately behind the farm buildings.

Description: There are 11 mounds spread out along the foot of the ward of Redland, of which 3 are close together near the farm. The largest, the northernmost of these 3, rises steeply to a height of about 9ft above a 'platform' about 3ft high. The platform is 93ft wide by about 79ft, the mound about 61ft by 55ft. When it was opened in 1858 a cist was found containing 4 gold 'sun discs', beads and pieces of amber as well as a cremation. All the cairns show signs of disturbance, but whether this is extensive in every case is dubious.

17 Maes Howe

NGR HY 318128

Location: About 9 miles W of Kirkwall, on the A965.

Description: Detailed description of this, the most famous megalithic tomb in Britain, is given on p 44f. Essentially it comprises a passage leading to a main chamber from which smaller mural cells open out, and is the type site for the 'Maes Howe' group of tombs. It was plundered by Vikings who carved runic inscriptions on many stones in the main chamber.

18   *Marwick*

NGR HY 229242

Location: In a field near the shore approached by the B9056 and a side road. The site is visible from the main road, and is about 3½ miles S of Birsay.

Description: A good example of an early chapel site, comprising a unicameral chapel, now visible as a low, turf-covered wall, about 17ft by 13ft (ie almost square), with a door with checked jambs on the south side. It lies within a sub-rectangular vallum, most of which can be traced. Features of the masonry suggest a Norse (twelfth-century) date, but the type has earlier antecedents.

19   *Netlater Broch*

NGR HY 323173

Location: Approached by the A986 and the same side road that leads to the Knowes of Trotty. The site adjoins Netlater buildings.

Description: About a third of the circumference of the broch wall is still standing, made of very large slabs. The inside wall stands about 6½ft high, the outside about 8ft. The wall is about 12ft thick, and enclosed an area about 33ft in diameter. It had three intra-mural chambers and a well. Outside were post-broch structures.

20   *Onstan (Unstan)*

NGR HY 283117

Location: About 2½ miles NE of Stromness, on the A965, near the shore of Loch of Stenness.

Description: This guardianship monument is a good example of an Orkney stalled cairn. Originally covered by an earth mound with three concentric walls, it is now covered by a Department of Environment concrete dome, like many other Orkney guardianship tombs. It has five compartments. When excavated, fragments of at least twenty-two 'Unstan' bowls were found.

21   Orphir—the Earl's Bu
NGR HY 334143
Location: Immediately adjoining the churchyard in which the round church stands.
Description: A few foundations are visible of a partly excavated complex of Norse buildings. Originally these probably covered a large area (there is evidence they extended as far as the nearby farm buildings), and belonged to an earl's palace mentioned in the *Orkneyinga Saga*.

22   Orphir Round Church
NGR HY 334043
Location: At Orphir, 8 miles WSW of Kirkwall, approached by the A964 and side road.
Description: Ruined chancel and part of the nave wall survive of this twelfth-century Norse church, probably ultimately modelled on the Church of the Holy Sepulchre in Jerusalem. It is the only surviving example of a round church of this period in Scotland (there may have been one at Old Roxburgh). What appears to be a twig rune can be seen on the outside chancel wall.

23   Quanterness
NGR HY 417129
Location: 3 miles from Kirkwall on the A965. The cairn is on the slopes of Wideford Hill, in the farmyard of Quanterness, visible from the road.
Description: The site now consists of a low mound, surmounted by a flagpole. When opened before 1805 it was found to consist of a passage at least 22ft long leading to a rectangular chamber 21ft 6in by 6ft 6in and 11ft 6in high. Six cells opened out from the chamber, arranged symmetrically.

The mound now stands to a height of about 10ft 6in and has a diameter of about 90ft. It was re-investigated in 1972.

24 Rennibister

NGR HY 397127

Location: About 4½ miles from Kirkwall, on the A965. The site lies in a farmyard.

Description: A good example of the Orcadian type of souterrain, comprising a passage and underground chamber with pillars supporting the roof. It is now in the guardianship of the Department of the Environment. It was found when a threshing machine broke the roof and contained, apart from black earth and shells, at least six human burials, presumably later than the main period of its use.

25 Ring of Bookan

NGR HY 282144

Location: Visible from the B9055 at Wasbuster, about 1 mile N of the Ring of Brodgar, at the north end of the isthmus separating Loch Stenness and Loch Harray.

Description: This now very ruined Maes Howe type of tomb shares with Maes Howe the feature of an enclosing ditch, which may represent an earlier 'henge'. This ditch is without an entrance, 44ft wide and 6ft deep, enclosing an area about 146ft wide. Stones lie in the centre of the enclosure, presumably the last vestiges of a tomb. Recently ploughed, the ditch is not clear for the whole of its circuit.

26 Ring of Brodgar

NGR HY 294134

Location: On the B9055, about 4 miles NE of Stromness, at the head of the isthmus separating Loch Harray and Loch Stenness.

Description: One of the finest circles of standing stones in the British Isles. Ranking with Callanish in Lewis or Avebury in Wiltshire, it now consists of a ditch with a subsidiary circle of 27 standing stones, all that remain out of about 60. The ditch of the earthwork is about 30ft wide and 6ft deep, while 1 stone stands to a height of 15ft and 6 others to over 10ft. The area enclosed is 120yd in diameter. Some stones bear runes, added by the later Norse. In the guardianship of the Department of the Environment.

27 Skara Brae

NGR HY 231188

Location: On the Bay of Skaill, about 6 miles NNW of Stromness, along the B9056. The site is approached by a path skirting the bay.

Description: One of the most famous prehistoric settlement sites in northern Europe, this site is discussed on p 6of. It comprises a group of sub-rectangular dwellings, complete with stone furniture, hearths and drains, with interconnecting passages. Occupied in the late Neolithic period. Now in the guardianship of the Department of the Environment, there is a site museum.

28 The Stenness-Brodgar complex

NGR Centring on HY 294134

Location: Centring on the Ring of Brodgar.

Description: The Ring of Brodgar and the Stenness Stones can be seen as two related henge monuments with associated stone circles, linking each side of the isthmus between Lochs Stenness and Harray. Between the two henges there can be seen the remains of a 'processional way' of standing stones in a single line. Four survive, and east of Stenness there is a fifth continuing the line. The most imposing is that known as the 'Watch Stone', which stands 18½ft high at HY 304128. Maes Howe, The Ring of Bookan and Unstan Cairn all lie within the Stenness area. Adjoining Bookan is a good disc-barrow at HY 287137, on the shore of Loch Harray, over 100ft in diameter and standing about 3ft high, while adjoining the Ring of Brodgar can be seen four further round barrows, one on the opposite side of the road from the modern entrance gate to the henge. There are further cairns between Brodgar and Bookan, and other standing stones in the area. Most of the cairns appear to have been plundered at some time or other.

29 The Stones of Stenness

NGR HY 306126

Location: On the B9055, about 1 mile S of the Ring of Brodgar, at the opposite end of the isthmus separating Lochs Stenness and Harray.

Description: The second of the two henge monuments of the Stenness-Harray complex, it consists of a ditch enclosing an area about 200ft in diameter, with an entrance in the north-west, and possibly another in the south-east, though this is not now clearly visible, due to the ditch being considerably ploughed out. Within the henge are set 4 stones, all that remain of a circle of originally about 13, probably about 105ft in diameter. One of the surviving stones stands 17ft high, 2 others over 15ft. A peculiar 'cromlech' or table of stones is a modern construction, erected in the belief that there should have been one on the site. In the guardianship of the Department of the Environment.

30 *Stones of Via*
NGR HY 259160
Location: Just off the A967, about ½ mile N of the Loch of Stenness. The site is just visible behind the farmhouse from the main road.
Description: A ruined chambered tomb, probably of Maes Howe type. A circular enclosure 61ft by 52ft is now barely visible, but seven large stones in the centre mark the remains of a burial chamber.

31 *Vestra Fiold*
NGR HY 238215
Location: On the slopes of Vestra Fiold, approached by the B9056 and A967, about 7 miles N of Stromness. The site can be reached by a farm road closed by a gate, and thence over rough ground.
Description: The site is that of a prehistoric quarry, used for quarrying blocks for chambered tombs or standing stones. A number of blocks lie embedded in the turf at intervals on the slope of Vestra Fiold, below the summit. One is propped up as though ready for moving. The stones for Maes Howe may have come from here.

32 *Wheelbin*
NGR HY 253263
Location: In a fenced-off field, on the A967, about 1 mile S of Birsay.
Description: A single standing stone, typical of the Orkney monuments of this type. It stands to a height of 12ft and leans slightly.

33 *Wideford Hill*

NGR HY 409122

Location: 2½ miles W of Kirkwall, along the A965. The site is near Cuween Hill, but slightly lower.

Description: A chambered tomb of Maes Howe type. The cairn material has been partly removed to expose three concentric retaining walls. The burial chamber has three large cells opening off it. The approach passage is not now used, the tomb is entered through a hatch inserted into the roof. Now in the guardianship of the Department of the Environment. It is unlikely the outer part of the approach passage was ever roofed. The main chamber was originally almost 10ft high, the upper part is now restored.

EDAY

34 *Sandyhill Smithy*

NGR HY 561327

Location: About 2 miles NNW of Backaland Pier, approached by the B9063.

Description: An Orkney-Cromarty tomb of stalled cairn type. It now appears as a grassy mound, 2ft high, from which three upright slabs protrude. It was excavated in 1937. The chamber was tripartite.

35 *Vinquoy Hill*

NGR HY 560382

Location: Towards the north side of the island, 5 miles NW of Backaland Pier.

Description: A Maes Howe type of tomb, now a conspicuous landmark on a ridge of moorland. It is overgrown with heather. The chamber is still preserved, approached by a passage 13ft long, and is polygonal, rising to a height of 9ft. Four chambers, in pairs, open off it.

CALF OF EDAY

36 *Calf of Eday Long*

NGR HY 579387

Location: 200yd from the west shore of Calf of Eday, a small islet lying off Eday.

Description: This is one of a group of chambered tombs on the Calf of Eday, the others being known as 'North-West' and 'South-East'. Calf of Eday Long, is a multi-period structure, a bipartite chambered building being incorporated into the cairn that was built to cover an Orkney-Cromarty stalled cairn, divided by partitions into four segments. Although overgrown, the main features can still be seen. The cairn is about 66ft long, the stalled chamber 23ft; the earlier structure, which may not have been funerary originally, is 10ft long. At some point in the Iron Age it was re-used, and occupation material was recovered from it.

EYNHALLOW

37   *Eynhallow Church*
NGR HY 359289
Location: Near the shore on Eynhallow.
Description: The ruins of a twelfth-century church, much altered in later times, and which at one stage served as a farmhouse. Adjoining it are the walls of domestic buildings of various periods, the majority probably date from the sixteenth century, but some may belong to an early monastery connected with the church. Now in the guardianship of the Department of the Environment.

HOY

38   *The Dwarfie Stane*
NGR HY 244005
Location: On the lower slopes of the Ward Hill, the highest hill in Orkney. Approached by the B9047 and side road, thereafter on foot.
Description: The only rock-cut chambered tomb in Britain, the Dwarfie Stane is a huge block of sandstone which has probably come from the cliffs above. It measures 28ft long and about 8ft high. A passage and two cells have been cut in it—the passage is 7ft 6in long and the cells about 5ft by 3ft. Passage and cells are only about 2ft 10in high. A blocking stone for the entrance lies nearby. The top has been badly mutilated by vandals, and the stone is covered with inscriptions, the earliest of which belongs to the early eighteenth century. One

appears to be in Arabic. In the guardianship of the Department of the Environment.

ROUSAY

39 Bigland Round
NGR HY 437325

Location: B9064 to the farm road leading to Bigland on the north-east of the island, thereafter on foot to the lowest terrace of Faraclett Head. It lies just above the limit of cultivation.

Description: A tripartite Orkney-Cromarty tomb, left open after excavation. All the features are clearly visible. The cairn was circular, about 40ft in diameter, with two wall faces, an external and an internal. The passage, only 3ft 10in long, is entered through portal stones, and was originally blocked with masonry. The tripartite chamber is 15ft 8in long.

40 Blackhammer
NGR HY 414276

Location: Just north of the B9064, 1½ miles W of Brinyan.

Description: A stalled cairn of Orcadian type, Blackhammer is now in the guardianship of the Department of the Environment, and covered with a concrete dome. It is unusual in that the entrance passage opens into the long side of the chamber, divided into seven compartments by septal slabs forming fourteen stalls. The chamber is 42ft 6in long and 6ft wide.

41 Knowe of Lairo
NGR HY 398279

Location: On the south side of the island, about 2½ miles from Brinyan Pier, near the B9064.

Description: A good example of an Orkney-Cromarty horned long cairn, the mound of which still survives to a length of 180ft. The entrance passage is 18ft long and opens out into a tripartite chamber about 17ft long; the walling of the chamber exists to a height of 13½ft, which is remarkable for a tomb of this type. There are considerable secondary alterations to the chamber which the intrepid can still enter along the passage.

42 Knowe of Yarso

NGR HY 403281

Location: 2 miles W of Brinyan Pier, along the B9064. Approached from the main road by a footpath.

Description: An Orkney-Cromarty stalled cairn, now in the guardianship of the Department of the Environment. It is virtually rectangular, about 50ft long by 25ft wide, the chamber being approached by a passage 13ft 2in long and divided up into four compartments by fairly low septal slabs which probably did not reach the roof. When excavated the compartments all showed traces of burning, and charred wood and ash was noted on the floor. The remains of twenty adults and one adolescent were recovered, as well as red deer, sheep and dog. Finds included Beaker and Food Vessel pottery and flints.

43 Midhowe Broch

NGR HY 371308

Location: On the shore on the west side of the island, approached by the B9064 and thence across rough pasture. It is about 4½ miles WNW of Brinyan Pier.

Description: Extensively excavated in the 1930s and now in the guardianship of the Department of the Environment, this broch with its attendant structures is a particularly good example. The broch itself is 30ft in diameter with a wall 15ft thick, which still stands 14ft high, the broch wall being made in two 'skins'. It stands in an enclosure with a wall and substantial quarry ditch on either side. There are secondary buildings clustered round the broch, as well as secondary slab partitions within it. The main features of broch architecture are almost all clearly discernible.

44 Midhowe Cairn

NGR HY 372306

Location: Adjoining Midhowe Broch.

Description: This unusually large stalled cairn of Orkney-Cromarty type is now in the guardianship of the Department of the Environment and encased in a hangar provided with gantries from which the details can be observed from above. It is 106ft long and 42ft wide, rectangular in plan, with a chamber no less than 76ft long divided up by septal slabs into twelve compartments. Low benches have been constructed in some of the compartments. The cairn has an inner and an outer casing, the latter faced with coursed slabs set herringbone fashion in a slant. The remains of twenty-five persons as well as numerous animal bones and sherds of Unstan-type pottery were recovered.

45 *Rinyo*
NGR HY 440321
Location: On the same terrace of Faraclett Head as Bigland Round, about 1 furlong to the south-east.
Description: Almost nothing is now visible of this village, which proved on excavation to be like Skara Brae, though the discerning may notice some low mounds in the turf.

46 *Taversoe Tuick*
NGR HY 426276
Location: About ¾ mile W of Brinyan Pier, near the B9064.
Description: Apart from Huntersquoy on Eday this is the only two-storeyed tomb in Scotland. It is a Bookan type of tomb, measuring 30ft in diameter, and the cairn is all of one build. The entrance to the upper chamber is oriented in the opposite direction to that for the lower, and the upper is constructed on the roof slabs of the lower. Four cells compose the compartments of the lower chamber, two the upper. A drain continues the line of the entrance passage to the lower chamber. Just beyond it is a miniature subterranean chamber, rock-cut and oval in plan, measuring 5ft by 3ft 10in and 2ft 10in high, now covered by a trap door. Among the finds were two complete Unstan bowls. The monument is now in the guardianship of the Department of the Environment.

47   *The Wirk*
NGR HY 375304
Location: About ¾ mile SE of Midhowe, farther along the shore.
Description: A stone tower, similar in dimensions to that of Cubbie
Roo's on Wyre. Essentially it is a square tower, with secondary later
walling. If the comparison with Cubbie Roo's is valid, it should date
from the twelfth century, but could be later. The secondary walling is
probably sixteenth century.

SANDAY
48   *Quoyness*
NGR HY 677378
Location: On the south coast of the island, 2 miles SSW of Roadside,
approached by the B9069 and side roads, thereafter on foot along the
headland.
Description: A tomb of Maes Howe type, which has been restored by
the Department of the Environment, in whose guardianship it is, to
show the retaining walls of the cairn in tiers, giving it a somewhat
'science fiction' appearance. It comprises a roughly rectangular
chamber, 13ft high, approached by a passage 12ft long. From the
main chamber six cells open out. The whole is erected on a platform,
which masked the entrance and the outermost wallface of the cairn—
entrance would have involved a drop into the passage.

WESTRAY
49   *Noltland Castle*
NGR HY 429488
Location: ½ mile NW of Pierowall.
Description: A sixteenth-century castle with a Z-plan—a type
developed to meet the requirements of firearms, with square towers at
each of two opposite corners. Built by Gilbert Balfour between 1560
and 1573, it was never completed.

PAPA WESTRAY

50 Knap o Howar

NGR HY 483519

Location: On the shore of the west side of Papa Westray, near Holland House.

Description: Two interconnected stone-built houses of sub-rectangular shape, which have been variously compared with Skara Brae, with early Iron Age houses and with post-broch huts. The finds were not very determinate, but suggest a Neolithic date.

51 St Tredwell's Chapel

NGR HY 496509

Location: On St Tredwell's Loch, near Cuppin, in the south of the island, approached by a side road.

Description: Situated on a peninsula which was probably an island in early Christian times, this site comprises a curved wall, probably the base of a broch, and a souterrain, probably belonging to a post-broch occupation period. The mound associated with these buildings is faced with a wall enclosing two small rectangular buildings, one a chapel similar in many respects to Marwick on Mainland, and presumably twelfth century, and an earlier building, perhaps an oratory. The dedication is to the Pictish saint, Triduana.

HOLM OF PAPA WESTRAY

52 Holm of Papa Westray Cairn

NGR HY 509518

Location: On the east side of this small uninhabited island.

Description: A tomb of Maes Howe type, now in the guardianship of the Department of the Environment, and covered with the usual Orcadian concrete dome, provided with access manhole. There are two tombs on the island, this, the south, is the better preserved and more interesting. It represents the most developed Maes Howe type, with a passage leading to the side of a long chamber, divided into three sections by two projecting masses of masonry, with fourteen cells opening out of the walls. The tomb is notable for its fine array of pecked carvings.

WYRE
53 Cubbie Roo's Castle
NGR HY 442264

Location: On the centre of the island, approached by a farm road.

Description: Probably one of the earliest stone castles in Scotland, the first phase of this monument may be an earth ringwork, in the centre of which is a stone tower, built by Kolbein Hruga (Cubbie Roo is a corruption) about 1145. The tower is rectangular, with a central well. It is surrounded by later, subsidiary structures.

54 St Mary's Chapel
NGR HY 443264

Location: Within sight of Cubbie Roo's castle.

Description: A late twelfth-century ruined chapel comprising nave and chancel, contemporary with Cubbie Roo's castle.

SHETLAND

The majority of the sites in the following list are on Mainland, and relatively easy of access. St Ninian's Isle can be reached on foot at low tide from the mainland. Although Mousa is uninhabited, a ferry service operates from Sandwick to take visitors to the broch. Being the two largest islands after Mainland, Yell and Unst have regular connecting ferry services. The other islands on which there are sites listed below can be reached directly by boat from the Mainland; a boat can usually be hired for the occasion as in most cases there are no regular ferries.

MAINLAND
1 Busta
NGR HU 349674

Location: In the north-west of the island, approached by the A970, situated on a cliff about 4½ miles NW of Voe.

Description: This is the most impressive of the few standing stones to be seen in Shetland. It is a granite pillar of roughly square section, and stands 10½ft above ground level. It probably dates from the early Bronze Age.

2 Clickhimin

NGR HU 465408

Location: On the outskirts of Lerwick, it can be approached by foot along the A970 from the town centre, and stands on a peninsula projecting into the Loch of Clickhimin. It is now in the guardianship of the Department of the Environment.

Description: This complex site is discussed at some length in the text (see p 102f). The earliest occupation on the site appears to belong to the late Bronze Age (c 700–500 BC) when a farmhouse was built. Early in the Iron Age the site was fortified with a stone fort with associated internal timber ranges, and a 'blockhouse' was also constructed. This is now one of the most striking features of the site. At a later date in the Iron Age a broch was built, which still stands to a height of over 17ft. Following the decay of the broch, there was continuing occupation on the site in the later Iron Age 'wheelhouse' period, ending probably shortly before the arrival of the Norse. Remains of most of the structural phases are still visible, and visitors should not forget to look at the footmarked stone set up near the entrance.

3 Clumlie

NGR HU 397185

Location: In the south of the island, some 15 miles S of Lerwick. The site lies about 45yd E of the main road (A968), some 500yd S of the junction of the Clumlie side road.

Description: This is a typical example of the Shetland Neolithic house sites. It appears as a depression enclosed by a grass-covered bank, now no more than about 18in high, from which earthfast stones protrude. It measures 45ft by 36ft overall. It has not been excavated.

4 Fort Charlotte

NGR HU 476418

Location: In Lerwick, overlooking the harbour.

Description: A good example of a seventeenth-century artillery fortification, roughly pentagonal with corner bastions. The walls are furnished with seaward gun loops. It was begun in 1665 to protect Bressay Sound, and was designed by Mylne, the king's master mason. It was burned by the Dutch when they sacked Lerwick in 1673, but repaired in the late eighteenth century. It is in the guardianship of the Department of the Environment.

5 Hill of Dale
NGR HU 409699
Location: Not far from the A968, about 4 miles N of Voe in the northwest of the island, on the saddle of the Hill of Dale.
Description: A good example of a Shetland heel cairn, of which the outline is well preserved. The façade of flanking stones, over 23ft long, is well preserved, but obscured to some extent by cairn material, and is without an entrance break. The cairn is now only a few feet high. Excavation in 1935 failed to reveal any internal chamber, possibly because the interior had been disturbed in antiquity.

6 Jarlshof
NGR HU 398096
Location: On Sumburgh Head, the most southerly tip of Shetland, it is within easy walking distance of Sumburgh airport.
Description: One of the most important archaeological sites in the British Isles, Jarlshof is discussed extensively in the appropriate chapters in the book. The site was occupied by a late Bronze Age/early Iron Age village, a later Iron Age settlement, a broch, a 'wheelhouse' period settlement, a sequence of Norse farmsteads, a medieval farmhouse and a seventeenth-century laird's house. The site is named after the fictional house in Scott's novel *The Pirate*. It has been extensively excavated, most recently by J. R. C. Hamilton after World War II (1949–52), and is in the guardianship of the Department of the Environment. There is a small museum on the site.

7 March Cairn
NGR HU 223789
Location: The cairn is situated in rough ground in a prominent posi-

tion on a ridge called the Hamars of Houlland, 4 miles WNW of Hillswick in the north-west of the island. It is approached by the A970 and B9078, and thence by foot.

Description: Although one of the Zetland group of cairns, it is rectangular or square in plan, measuring approximately 33ft in each direction. It now stands about 3ft high, and its structural features are visible, following excavation in 1949. A passage runs from behind the centre of the south-east side of the cairn to a chamber with a recess at each side and at the rear. The cairn is edged with large rectangular facing stones.

8   *Nesbister Hill*
NGR HU 403454
Location: On top of Nesbister Hill, 5 miles NW of Lerwick, approached by the A970 and A971.
Description: This cairn is circular in plan, and measures 26ft in diameter. In the centre of the cairn is a stone cist, 4ft by about 2½ft wide, with a partly displaced capstone. The cairn is notable for its well-built kerb wall. It is uncertain whether it is Neolithic or later.

9   *Ness of Burgi*
NGR HU 388084
Location: At Scatness on the tip of Sumburgh, about a mile SW of Jarlshof, from which it can be reached on foot by an attractive walk along the headland.
Description: Now very ruinous, this is a type of promontory fort, defended by two ditches cutting off the promontory, with a stone wall about 21ft thick and 7ft high between them. On the inner lip of the inner ditch is the 'blockhouse', a structure akin to that at Clickhimin, pierced by a central entrance and with lateral guard cells. It dates from the earlier Iron Age. It is in the guardianship of the Department of the Environment.

10   *Ness of Gruting*
NGR HU 280483
Location: Situated about 2¾ miles SE of Bridge of Walls in the west of

the island, and approached by the A971 and a side road. The site is best approached from Upper Gruniquoy.

Description: There are a group of five houses at the Ness of Gruting, of which the Ness of Gruting itself has been excavated. It is oval in shape, and comprises a room with an apsidal end chamber leading off. The chamber was about 30ft long by 20ft wide, the apsidal annexe 5ft by 10ft. The walls were about 10ft thick. At a secondary stage the size of the main room was reduced and a new apse constructed. The site is notable for producing abundant finds, including 28lb of charred barley and a great quantity of pottery—it housed a potter's workshop. Associated with the houses are field boundaries and clearance cairns. The site was occupied in the Neolithic period.

11   *Punds Water*
NGR HU 324712
Location: This site can be approached by A970, and is about 7½ miles NW of Voe in the north-east of the island. It is situated in particularly wild moorland, and access involves an arduous walk.

Description: Along with Vementry this is one of the most impressive of the Shetland heel cairns. It is built of white quartzite boulders, rising to a height of about 5ft above the surrounding terrain. The façade is over 50ft wide with substantial walling, and there is a wall delimiting the cairn. The entrance to the burial chamber is in the centre of the façade, and both the approach passage and the chamber itself are now open to the air. It was cleared in 1930.

12   *Ronas Hill*
NGR HU 305834
Location: In the north of the island, 5 miles NNE of Hillswick, approached by the A970. The cairn is situated near the top of Ronas Hill, the highest point in Shetland.

Description: The site is badly disturbed, and the edge difficult to determine due to being overgrown, but was at least 45ft in diameter. It may originally have been a heel cairn, is now over 10ft high, but may have been built up in the centre in recent times. In it a passage and rectangular burial chamber can still be seen.

13   Sae Breck

NGR HU 210780

Location: In the north of the island, 4½ miles E by N of Hillswick, approached by the A970 and B9078. It crowns the hill called Sae Breck.

Description: A typical broch tower, now reduced to a mound of stones, but originally about 25ft in diameter with walls about 15ft thick. Two intra-mural chambers are discernible—one yielded a considerable quantity of pottery. The entrance was probably on the east side.

14   Scalloway Castle

NGR HU 405393

Location: In Scalloway, overlooking the harbour.

Description: Built in 1600 by Patrick Stewart, Earl of Orkney, this is a good example of a late type of tower house built on the 'two-stepped' plan. It has a particularly fine staircase. In the guardianship of the Department of the Environment.

15   Selli Voe

NGR HU 295484

Location: In the north-west of the island, above the head of Selli Voe in the south end of the Walls peninsula. It is not very far from the Ness of Gruting, and can be approached by a similar route.

Description: An example of a Neolithic heel cairn, though little of the cairn material is still surviving. Much of the kerb can still be traced. The cairn had a passage terminating in a rectangular chamber within it, now represented by six slabs. The façade is 24ft long.

16   Stanydale House

NGR HU 288503

Location: The approach route to Stanydale Temple leads past this site, which is on the moorland somewhat closer to the road.

Description: This is a good example of the Shetland type of Neolithic house, and has been excavated. It is one of a group of five houses with associated fields, and there are others not far away. The 'temple' is presumed to relate to them. The house is oval, about 30ft by 15ft internally, and has a main chamber, with two recesses, and an almots circular inner room. The entrance to the house is protected by a curved 'porch'. A bench is visible within the house, and associated with the building, but probably of later date, is a drystone enclosure.

17 Stanydale 'Temple'

NGR HU 285503

Location: In the west of the island, 1½ miles ESE of Bridge of Walls, it is approached by the A971 and a side road. It is signposted, and is reached by a moderate walk over the moorland.

Description: This remarkable Neolithic site is heel-shaped in plan, and in this respect resembles the heel cairns. The wall is built of substantial undressed blocks, enclosing an oval about 40ft by 20ft across, the wall averaging 12ft thick. It is entered through a passage in the curved façade. The rear of the chamber has six shallow recesses. On excavation, two post holes were found, possibly for roof supports, containing vestiges of spruce, a wood not native to Scotland and which may have come as driftwood from America. Its function is unknown. It is now in the guardianship of the Department of the Environment.

FETLAR

18 Haltadans

NGR HU 623924

Location: This is 3 miles inland from Ugasta Pier, the landing point on Fetlar, and is approached by the B9088 and thereafter on foot over the moorland.

Description: A cairn of presumably Bronze Age date, consisting of a ring of upright slabs, 37ft in diameter, set edge to edge, with a gap in the south-west which may be an original feature. Within this enclosure there is a low bank concentric with it, also with a gap in the south-west. In the centre are two earthfast boulders.

MOUSA

19   *Broch of Mousa*
NGR HU 457237
Location: On the west shore of the island, facing the Mainland.
Description: The best preserved of the Scottish broch towers, Mousa
still rises to a height of about 43ft, the top can still be approached by
the intra-mural staircases. A scarcement for an internal timber range
is visible within the broch, which has a central well and post-broch
secondary structures within it. In the guardianship of the Department
of the Environment.

ST NINIAN'S ISLE

20   *St Ninian's Isle Chapel*
NGR HU 367207
Location: On the tidal St Ninian's Isle off the west coast of the Mainland. Approached by the A970 and B9122, thence on foot from the
main road overland and across a spit of sand at low tide. The site is on
the shore facing the Mainland.
Description: This is the site of the discovery of the St Ninian's Isle
Treasure, which was found near the southern chancel arch of the
church. The present remains are confusing due to the building of
retaining walls for spoil during the excavation, which are difficult to
distinguish from the ancient remains. Structures of different periods
are visible. The church with apse and chancel is not earlier than the
twelfth century. In the early Christian period the site appears to have
been no more than a developed cemetery. Part of the enclosure wall
perhaps belongs to this period, and adjoining the chapel is what has
been interpreted as a 'founder's tomb'.

UNST

21   *Burra Ness*
NGR HU 556956
Location: 2¼ miles S by E of Gutcher, on Burra Ness facing Unst and
Fetlar. Approached by a farm road then by foot across the moorland.
Description: A particularly fine example of a broch, which still stands

to a height of 12ft on the interior which is 27ft in diameter. The walls are 15ft thick. The scarcement ledge on the interior is still visible.

22 Muckle Heog West
NGR HP 630108
Location: It is 1¼ miles NE of Baltasound. Approached by the A968 and thence over the moorland. The Muckle Heog is a hill crowned with four cairns.
Description: The topmost cairn on the hill, Muckle Heog East, is badly ruined. Muckle Heog West is situated slightly to the west of it, on the saddle 50ft below the summit. It too has been badly disturbed, but was a heel cairn of Shetland type. The cairn rises to a height of about 3½ft, and the façade which is slightly curved is 41½ft across. In the cairn can be seen two stone cists, set at ground level. Two others were noted in the last century but are not now visible.

23 Muness Castle
NGR HP 629013
Location: On the south of the island, not far from the ferry jetty.
Description: The most northerly castle in the British Isles, Muness is dank and forbidding. It was rubble-built in the late sixteenth century on the Z-plan, and its most striking feature is the presence of considerable numbers of gun loops. It has some notable architectural detail. Now in the guardianship of the Department of the Environment.

24 The Rounds of Tivla
NGR HP 615107
Location: On moorland on Crussa Field, 1¼ miles N of Baltasound.
Description: Three cairns with low concentric stony banks enclosing a central mound. The best preserved has a mound 13ft in diameter, enclosed by three rings, 30, 40 and 53ft in diameter respectively. The innermost appears to be of earth with a quarry ditch, the others of stone. The type of site has Bronze Age affinities, but precise parallels are not known.

25   *Uyea Breck*
NGR HP 605606
Location: 1 mile E of Uyeasound, 100yd S of the Muness road.
Description: This is one of the very few standing stones in Shetland, and rises to a height of 10ft above ground. It is a monolithic pillar of schist.

VEMENTRY
26   *Vementry Cairn*
NGR HU 294610
Location: Separated from the Mainland by a channel 200yd wide at its narrowest point. The island can be approached by land from Voe, and thence by boat. The site is on top of the highest hill, the Muckle Ward.
Description: This is the finest of the Shetland heel cairns. It is composed of a heel-shaped platform, surmounted by a circular cairn enclosing a chamber. The façade is 36ft across, well preserved, without a break, composed of large slabs set on end. The cairn, which is of one build with the platform, has a trefoil-shaped chamber approached by a passage 12ft long.

WHALSAY
27   *The Benie Hoose* (or *Bunyie Hoose*)
NGR HU 586652
Location: Side road to Isbister and thereafter by foot across the moorland. The site is on Pettigarths Field, north-east of Alma.
Description: A typical example of the Shetland Neolithic house, this site has a forecourt to the dwelling proper. It has a figure-of-eight plan, and measures 8oft in length, the main block being 42ft wide and comprising a main chamber with two side recesses. The walls now stand to a height of about 4ft. It was excavated 1954–6 and interpreted, without real reason, as the dwelling of officiating priests at the nearby Stones of Yoxie.

28   *Isbister—The Gairdie*
NGR HU 584646
Location: 3 miles NE of Symbister, almost due south of the Benie

Hoose, approached by the Isbister farm road and thereafter on foot overland.

Description: Locally known as the Gairdie, this consists of a house with three terminal apses. The house is oval in shape, and the main chamber is about 23ft long. The central apse is about 10ft across, and has what appears to be the base of a stone-built dresser. It was tested with a trial trench, and produced some stone tools of a type familiar on the Neolithic house sites.

29   *The Loch of Huxter*
NGR HU 558620
Location: Situated on an island in the Loch of Huxter, 1¼ miles E of Symbister, and which is approached by by-roads and thence over the moorland.

Description: The island on which the site stands is joined to the shore by a man-made causeway. The site is a good example of an early Iron Age stone fort, and is comparable in its position to Clickhimin. The fort consists of a stone wall enclosing an area about 70ft across, entered through a 'blockhouse' of Clickhimin type, 41ft long by 21ft wide as at Clickhimin, with two flanking guard chambers. There may have been a cell in the fort wall, but this is not certain.

30   *The Standing Stones of Yoxie*
NGR HU 586652
Location: 100yd E of the Benie Hoose.
Description: Believed by the excavator to be a 'temple' like Stanydale, Yoxie in plan is similar to the nearby Benie Hoose. A courtyard leads to the main structure, in which the main chamber has a slightly smaller annexe with an apsidal recess at the far end. The whole is of figure-of-eight plan, measuring about 61ft by 36ft overall. The entrance to the main chamber is afforded by a passage way through the wall which is about 15ft thick at this point. The absence of querns and other domestic artifacts suggests that it was not a normal house.

WEST BURRA

31 *Papil Kirkyard*

NGR HU 368315

Location: Adjoining the jetty at Papil.

Description: The modern graveyard wall is built on the vallum of an earlier period, presumably that of the early Christian monastery. There is evidence to suggest the site is that of an important monastery. The shell of the now derelict church stands on a mounded area (the church dates from 1815) and below the floor are visible fragments of masonry of an earlier structure. Fragments of corner-post shrines were found on the site.

YELL

32 *Burgi Geos*

NGR HP 477034

Location: On a high promontory, 5 miles NE of Gutcher, approached over 3½ miles of moorland north-west from Dalsetter.

Description: An Iron Age stone fort of the same general type as the Ness of Burgi and the Loch of Huxter. It is defended by a wall of independently set stones, behind which is set a 'blockhouse' wall about 35ft long and 13ft thick.

Acknowledgements

It gives me pleasure to record here the help I have had from a number of friends and colleagues who put at my disposal the results of their unpublished work. Among these I would single out for special thanks Dr Anna Ritchie, who provided me with information on her excavation at Buckquoy; Mr David Clarke, for an account of the recent excavations at Skara Brae; and Mr Peter Gelling, for details of his work at Skaill. I owe a special debt to T. G. E. Powell who read Professor the manuscript in its entirety, offering useful suggestions. I owe particular thanks to Miss Michele Elford and Mr David Longley for redrawing many of my rough sketches for this book. Finally, my students helped me in checking out details of sites on the ground for the gazetteer.

SOURCES OF THE ILLUSTRATIONS

Plates 1b, 3b, 4b, 5b, 14, and 15a are reproduced by courtesy of the Department of the Environment, Crown Copyright Reserved. Plates 9, 10 and 13 are reproduced by courtesy of the National Museum of Antiquities of Scotland, Edinburgh. The other photographs are by the author, with the exception of 12b, kindly supplied by Dr Anna Ritchie.

All the line drawings have been produced specifically for this book. The following are based, however, on published illustrations, the sources for which are given.

5,7 After S. Piggott, *Neolithic Cultures of the British Isles* (1954), Fig 37.

ACKNOWLEDGEMENTS

6   After R.C.H.A.M.S., *Inventory of Orkney*, Fig 351.
8   After *Inventory of Orkney*, Fig 382.
9   After Piggott, *Neolithic Cultures*, Fig 37.
15 After R.C.H.A.M.S., *Inventory of Orkney*, Fig 348.
17 After Calder in F. T. Wainwright (ed), *The Northern Isles* (1962),
    Fig 9.
18 After Calder, *op cit*, Fig 14.
24 After *Inventory of Orkney*, Fig 374.
25 After *Introduction to the Inventory of Orkney and Shetland*, Fig
    10.
29 After J. R. C. Hamilton, *Excavations at Jarlshof* (1956), Fig 10.
33 After J. R. C. Hamilton, *Excavations at Clickhimin* (1968), Fig 11.
39 After *Inventory of Orkney*, Fig 129.
40 After *Inventory of Orkney*, Fig 273.
43 After *Inventory of Orkney*, Fig 232.
45 After Hamilton, *Excavations at Jarlshof*, Fig 90.
50 After *Inventory of Orkney*, Fig 328.
53 After A. C. Thomas, *The Early Christian Archaeology of North
    Britain* (1972), Fig 73.
59 After Hamilton, *Excavations at Jarlshof*, Fig 63.
64 After *Inventory of Orkney*, Fig 258.
66 After *Inventory of Orkney*, Fig 325.
67 After Hamilton, *Excavations at Jarlshof*, Fig 86.
68 After S. H. Cruden, *The Scottish Castle* (1962), Figs 23 and 25.
69 After *Inventory of Orkney*, Fig 215.

I am grateful to the National Museum of Antiquities of Scotland
for allowing me to publish drawings of unpublished material from
Birsay, which appear as Fig 52.

L. L.

Index

Page numbers in italics indicate illustrations